JOURNEY TO THE SOURCE

NICK SANDERS

Photography by
Ian Woollams
and
Nick Sanders

ACKNOWLEDGEMENTS

I should like to thank most gratefully the following people for assisting me in the production of this book and my journey leading up to it.

Mr John Nichols, Sales and Marketing Director of Vimto plc for his generous support along with Group Sales Director, Mr Alan Isherwood. Mr Bob Harris, Press and PR Manager of Air France UK for kindly assisting the passage of myself and my photographer to Cairo. Meridien Hotels for supporting me on the return leg of the journey. Raleigh for their kind support and for supplying the bike.

Mr Dermody, John, Brian, Ann and Vivienne of 'Woodheys Farm Restaurant' in Glossop for their helpful support and lovely meals. Mr Mike Parsons, John Lewis and Derek Draper of Karrimor in Accrington for providing the panniers. Stan and Mrs Hughes of Gibbsport in Salford for their super jerseys. Steve Scutt at 'Striders' in Loughborough for their 880 track suits. Graham Smith at Le Coq Sportif UK in Holmes Chapel for supplying cycling shoes and the Stockport Express/Advertiser for so generously supplying all the film. To Pan Books for allowing me to use a quote from 'Dispatches' by Michael Herr; Rudyard Kipling Estate; Spike Milligan and Faber & Faber.

On a more personal level it has taken over three years before I could be in a position to complete a journey of this nature and I should like to thank the following people for their friendship, help and unselfish support.

Roy, Monty and the Chisholm family in Canterbury. Geoff and Rosemary Newson. Simon Cole and Tim Grundy, also Susy Mathis at Piccadilly Radio. Francesca Thomson at the Air France Telex for keeping contact throughout the journey and Jane Jones, Bob Harris's PA for all the cups of coffee. Alastair MacDonald at Look North West for his consistent help. Jennifer Whitelaw and Nigel Martin at Prosper Communications in Bolton for their fabulous support. Ian for taking photographs even though he nearly died from Malaria, well done Ian! David Hume, Diana Stenson and Christopher Walmsley for the kind encouragement. To Guy Mailer at the Manchester Evening News for continued interest and to Peter Stansfield of Barclays Bank in Leeds for having confidence in me.

Also John Senior at the Transport Publishing Company in Glossop for his enthusiasm and to Ray Eatock of 'A' Design for designing the book in an incredible two weeks. I should also like to thank Fares of Cairo, the British Council in Cairo and Brothers Elliot and Joe at Locar.

I also wish to thank Tom and Ellen Bowers and John and Vivienne Bouchier for their friendship and also for their constant support right from the beginning. To Vivienne for typing the manuscript, acting as my PA and for generally keeping everything together and lastly my father and late mother for being so incredibly patient with their eccentric son.

INTRODUCTION

It takes a while to achieve the right frame of mind to travel, and at the end of a journey it requires as much will power to return home. Looking over Lake Tanganyika and the jungles of Zaire, I can't help thinking that whenever I read about the great adventurous exploits ascending Everest or crossing the North Pole, I along with most people was amazed at the courage needed and the great imagination necessary. When I set off around the world with my borrowed £700 it never occurred to me that I too would become a traveller, adventurer or as you like explorer, it all seemed fairly mysterious and hard.

Having completed four long journeys, one of which ascended to Everest Base Camp, the journeying remained arduous as ever but has of late become a way of life. I have always maintained that if I could cross the Nubian Desert, Uganda, the Sinai or the Himalayas, then so could most people. I like to think of exploration as something one would actually choose to do, quite unrelated with awe and bravado.

It is very difficult for me to assess the validity of my journey to the source of the Nile and I am sure that as there are many people who admire it there will be those who think it absurd.

Financially all my journeys have a budget of £1.50 a day and apart from a tape recorder and tapes all I carry is a spare tyre, mosquito net, spare jersey and shorts, a toothbrush, one map, a camera, and a note-pad and pen. Nothing else.

Meridien Hotel, Source du Nil
Bujumbura

Nick Sanders

Nick Sanders was born on 26th November 1957 in Bradford, a working class area of Manchester, where he spent his childhood. Having a very competitive nature he became schoolboy cycling champion after which he decided to embark on a professional cycling career and went to live near Paris. An accident unfortunately curtailed an interesting future in the sport whereupon he commenced his studies at Loughborough University. During University he deferred a year and worked as a barman to save up enough money to cycle round the world. Nick presently appears in the Guinness Book of Records as the fastest man ever to complete such a journey.

Nick has visited over forty countries in the last three years, and as well as being a freelance writer and broadcaster, he is also a fellow of the Royal Geographical Society. The author is not married, does not have two children and does not live in Surrey.

Ian Woollams

Ian is a freelance photographer living near Manchester and has worked in advertising photography for seven years. At 23 he is considered young to have travelled so widely and as well as pursuing his interests in the UK intends to journey extensively in the near future.

CONTENTS

For my mother

CAIRO... the beginning

Young man you have the whole world before you, and you have nothing. You must travel around the world, that is obligatory if only to realise what a futile and pointless act it is.

Fares of Cairo.

The stewardess gave me an extra 'petite' bottle of wine. She was French and charming, not used to cyclists flying to Egypt, particularly ones well mesmerised by copious quantities of St. Emilion after having decided to celebrate the start of an adventure. The Air France Boeing landed smoothly at Cairo International Airport taxi-ing into the terminus and I stepped off the plane knowing my journey to the source of the Nile had begun.

Quickly collecting my panniers and bike I was whisked through customs immediately and set off for a city packed with stuff dreams are made of, my dreams of a faraway Arabia. Along the desert road through gleaming Heliopolis and grimy inner city suburbs I'd reached the glossy inlaid life of Talaat Herbe, my reflection tripping full lick past innumerable shoe shop windows on both sides of the road. I was looking for a dirty yellow sign marked Golden Hotel and just above the street level smog it hung slightly askew.

This was Mister Fares' haven for travellers on the run, bog-eyed and lost, looking for a home for a night. I squeezed my bike upright in the cupboard he called a lift, two finger-worn wooden doors closed behind me creating Faustian confines until in silence I reached the fifth floor and Fares, seated on his sofa opposite his florid full-length mirror. Fares was an old friend from a previous visit to Cairo and he was, as ever, immaculate in his three-piece suit, eighty years if he was a day and Oxford educated, terribly proper and proud of it. He showed me a dormitory room scattered with travellers, all going somewhere, some coming back, and a few doing nothing.

Morning came and everyone who was going to Sudan was having problems obtaining a visa so I walked over to Garden City, to the Sudanese Embassy, breathing in the sweet decay of Cairo. Cairo for me was a mascara-laden lady with her loveliness painted finger nail deep and left on for a week to flake. Rouge was just a little too thick covering proud cheekbones on display, only later to peel. The traffic raced around the central square, Midan Tahrir and her hair was a little dishevelled, lips a little smudged but Cairo embraces you warmly.

On reaching the Embassy it appeared the visa for Sudan was going to present a problem. I managed to explain my predicament to one of the Ambassador's secretaries, Mr 'M', and he was very helpful but I had to ask the British Embassy to telex their counterpart in Khartoum to contact the Ministry of Foreign Affairs; they would then contact the Cairo office, it would only take a month or so. "I'm sorry," said Mr 'M', "but if and when you do reach Khartoum you will understand."

I walked back to Talaat Harb Square feeling very disheartened. In London the Sudanese Embassy had told me I would obtain my visa within three days in Cairo, obviously this would not be the case. I went into Groppies, not a flattering name for a cafe, the Cafe Royale of Arabia. One visioned a rapacious Cairo politician, crazed and a little mad, but inside the blur of traffic fractionally quietened. Cairo at my level of life was not a pleasant experience, but then pleasantries were never designed to appreciate carnal grime. Taffeta sunrises and perfumed sails blowing in the wind were quite another matter. At subsistence level, Cairo is a city of car horns, plagiarising thoughts, abducting imagination, the smash and grab of finer feelings. In time I was to love this city like no other, but my remaining here had still to be justified. The journey would be delayed a month and there was no way I could speed my visa.

"We have cafe au laith or ze thea, you want?" The old waiter spoke and balanced, both at the same time. I sat down, leaning on a small green formica-topped table, chipped at the edges, stained

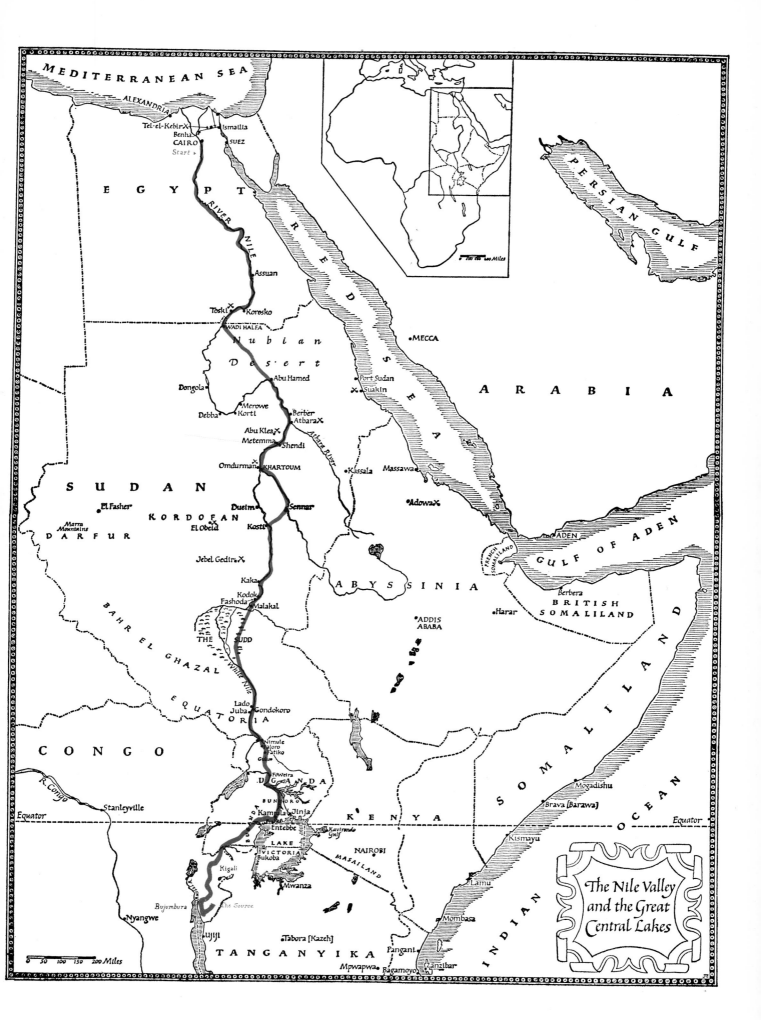

MEDITERRANEAN SEA

ALEXANDRIA
Tel-el-Kebir✕
Benha Ismailia
CAIRO SUEZ
Start

E G Y P T

RIVER NILE

Assuan

Toski✕ •Korosko
WADI HALFA

Nubian
Desert

Dongola
Debba Merowe Abu Hamed
Korti Berber Port Sudan
Atbara✕ ✕Suakin

R E D
S E A

•MECCA

A R A B I A

S U D A N

El Fasher• Abu Klea✕
Metemma Shendi
Omdurman✕ KHARTOUM

KORDOFAN Duem✕ Sennar
Marra El Obeid• Kosti
Mountains
D A R F U R

Jebel Gedir•✕

BAHR EL GHAZAL

Kaka
Kodok
Fashoda• Malakal

THE SUDD

EQUATORIA

Kassala• Massawa

Adowa✕•

A B Y S S I N I A

•ADDIS
ABABA

•Harar

ADEN
FRENCH
SOMALILAND GULF OF ADEN
Berbera
BRITISH
SOMALILAND

PERSIAN
GULF

C O N G O

R.Congo
Stanleyville

Equator

Lado
Juba Gondokoro
Nimule
Dufile
Fatiko
Gulu
Foweira
U G A N D A
BUNYORO
Kampala Jinja
Entebbe Kavirondo
Gulf

LAKE
VICTORIA
Bukoba

Kigali

Bujumbura The Source
Nyangwe•
UJIJI

T A N G A N Y I K A
Mpwapwa•

K E N Y A

MASAILAND

NAIROBI•

Mwanza

•Tabora [Kazeh]
Pangani•
Bagamoyo•

S O M A L I L A N D

Mogadishu•
•Brava [Barawa]

Equator

Kismayu•

Lamu•

Mombasa•

Zanzibar

I N D I A N

O C E A N

0 50 100 150 200 Miles

0 100 200 200 Miles

The Nile Valley
and the Great
Central Lakes

nine

with use. Patiently waiting, the waiter's jaw proceeded to compress the rest of his face, nimble gums replacing teeth, speech was slurped; "wiv wather ......" Between his face-eating chin and his red plant pot fez poked a nose and two eyes, dull with age marking time. I told him I wanted milk, coffee and croissants with butter and jam to compensate for being here. Such compensation would only last a while.

The positiveness of the journey had gone because my plans were like sediment and hadn't yet settled. Everything was so vague, unsure; what if my entry were to be refused, if I were refused permission to cycle? I couldn't return home and go elsewhere. As with all insecure steps forward, as opposed to those that step back, to return from a journey empty-handed would hallmark the next with doubt.

The journey hadn't quite started but the adventure was well into its stride, but what would happen if the waiting made the journey impotent? A chapter heading perhaps, Atrophy of an Adventure. Now I was smiling, I felt like a lonely realist in a society of cloud cuckoos. Old Abdul arrived, heaving stainless steel jugs with milk and coffee, croissants oozing with butter, and a saucerful of jam to spread. It was mid-day and I hadn't eaten; goodness knows why croissants, my whole daily allowance spent on flimsy French pastry.

Next morning I went to shower then someone tapped me on the shoulder; "Ah yes, good morning, care for a cup of tea?" I looked around to see an Asian fellow, tea-stained in his green striped pyjamas. "It is such that I am Mohammed, we live here, oh yes we do." He pointed to an open doorway, "It would be a great honour if you would join us, please your name." I told him. "Ah Mr Terry it is such that we have a Mr Nicholas for tea", and at that he gently tutted, paused a moment and led me into the room. Tea making paraphernalia was scattered on newspaper to my left as I peered through the door; a huge Victorian mirror hung above. Further along the wall a Biblical sculptured oak panel was partly obscured by an Arabesque wall-hanging, there were four beds and on the one by the wall sat Terry. "Terry, wake up, we have a guest, Mr Nicholas has come to see us. This is Mr Terry", he said turning to me, and with that Mohammed bowed almost imperceptibly with the good grace of a man of position. "Yes, er, well yes, what a surprise. English, yes, ah well, do take a seat, tea perhaps, hmm ......" I liked Terry immediately. He claimed to be the original nine stone weakling, or, as he put it, eight and a half, his nose bearing the full weight of his square metal-rimmed glasses and a Louis XIVth beard grimly stuck on the end of his pointed chin. "Cycling, how um extraordinary", and he, like Mohammed, bowed but more nervously as he took a slight step back to compensate. I talked for most of the evening with Terry, a forty-eight year old ex-antique dealer from Cambridge. "Knick-knacks and bric-a-brac, that kind of rubbish," he said. He'd left his wife to travel the world and sort of got stuck in Cairo these last twelve months. Mohammed punctuated the conversation with tuts at random intervals, arms crossed, head cocked forward and with glazed interest would say "Really Mr Nicholas," and I knew that Mr would be replaced before long with a contempt for youth and youthful bravado. It was agreed I rent a quarter of a room for a month, we shook hands and I was to move in the very next night.

Every morning I walked over to Garden City and the Sudanese Embassy where telexes had been sent — still no reply from Khartoum. Every day, usually on the way back, Terry and I would rest awhile in the American University just off Tahrir Square. The University garden was laden with whicker basket tables and chairs, plastic mugs of coffee and refectory sticky buns for breakfast. Such was luxury as the early morning sun filtered through the fountain spray and pepper-green beech trees tinkle-rustling breezily above student talk, putting the world to rights.

Terry was a compulsive talker, he talked when he wanted and he talked when he didn't and when he talked he smoked. Cleopatra and Nefertiti were his favourite brands, they being the cheapest. I often chided him for wasting so much money. He hoped to get to India - he'd be lucky to get out of Egypt! He was the most indecisive fellow I had ever met whose life was a continuous series of nervous movements, erratic motion in progress, twitching from one idea to the next. "Well I suppose umm, I could go to Mombasa, get a dow to Bombay or Karachi", he paused but then he always paused, "Overland to Delhi, perhaps, Kathmandu perhaps, or maybe not perhaps". Terry prattled in linked continuous spurts, an arrangement he'd come to terms with and if nobody listened it didn't make any difference. "Port Sudan and over to Yemen, I suppose I could go via Israel, Syria, Turkey ...... " My thoughts drifted gently, Terry's drone wasn't unpleasant and if I said blandly and in the most uninteresting manner possible, "That's a good idea Terry', he'd stop and think, rather pleased with someone thinking he was even capable of good ideas, although he knew himself he wasn't. " Oh well umm, thanks, umm, yes well, er I suppose I could do that," and he started to think as to whether he could or not.

We discussed routes, walked around town and ended up in the spice bazaar near the market at Khan el Khalili just off Sharia Muizz, south of the Madrasa of Qalaun. Every dressing and seasoning imaginable was stored in glass jars by the thousand. Pickled vegetables, chutney and sandy jars of Dijon mustard; cayenne and chilli, capsicum, paprika and pimento; tangy red peppers, cinnamon and saffron, galingale and ginger, nutmeg and clove. Fragrances awning the alleyways to life.

Several areas of Cairo, even Talaat Harb's commerciality portrayed smells and sounds quite their own, but Khan el Khalili was quite the most distinctive. Tiny, poky stone-walled shops facing each other across the narrow chaotic alley. A midaq alley. Market areas are notoriously amorphic, motley, where people are the placemats on a mosaic-tiled pavement. The atmosphere here was a step out of time, anachronistic, unshaven, breathing in the dust of ages but so rich, so vibrant and alive. Sacks of dirty-white tick-ridden wool next to trollies piled high with black, shiny olives. Crates of chickens alongside the cackle of geese and golden cow brand palm oil from Jurang Park Road, Singapore. Pure butter ghee from Karachi and black Singer sewing machines from Glasgow. People, people everywhere, every other person smiles, the children race by laughing to shout 'welcome' in Egypt. A pretty little girl tugs my shirt and grins, wiping her nose with the back of her hand. Then, dry cleaning it on the sleeve of her pale straw yellow frock, she runs off, laughing gleefully, a last look behind as she disappears through a crack in the wall.

Friday is, of course, the Islamic day of rest and Groppies for coffee was the nearest I could get to that Sunday morning paper feeling back home. I never consciously try to re-live home life, travelling is an attitude of mind where one's mind must travel too and if thoughts are always with family and friends one is simply going through the motions, adhering to procedure. It's all a question of absorption. Today, without the stampede of cars, the hustling, the voices, the jungle, there was a slight feeling of sanity. Finches were chirping above, flirting about, perched on telephone wires, hopping and bobbing, chatting; preening their feathers to

Nile Explorers I

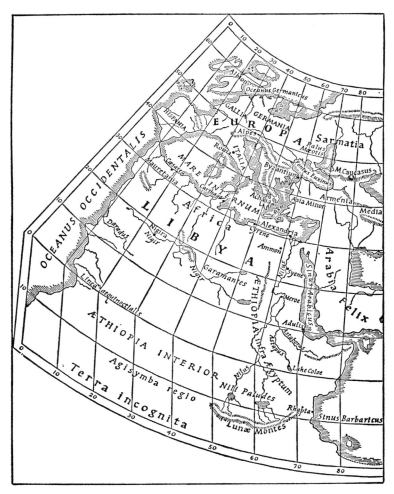

The map of Africa taken from Ptolemy's Map of the World.

The early journeys along the Nile were really something more than mere exploration. In the deserts the river was life itself and if, even for one season it failed to flow then Egypt would have perished. Herodotus ascended the Nile in 460BC and reached the first cataract at Aswan. Even Nero sent a small expedition into the Sudan having been blocked in the far interior by an unpenetrable swamp. One of the most persistent legends about the Source of the Nile related to the travels of a Greek merchant in the middle of the first century AD, Diogenes. Journeying overland from a settlement called Rhapta, a little north of Zanzibar, Diogenes said he had 'travelled inland for twenty-five days journey and arrived in the vicinity of two great lakes, to see the snowy range of mountains whence the Nile draws its twin sources.'

This is the story recorded by the Syrian geographer Marinus of Tyre, and it was from the records or Marinus that Ptolemy produced in the middle of the second century his map of the world.

It wasn't until 1848 that new information was to reach the Royal Geographical Society in London. Johann Rebmann, one of the earliest missionaries in Africa used a similar route to Diogenes and produced a report which claimed the siting of a large mountain called Kilimanjaro. Furthermore, to be received with great ridicule, the report claimed it had snow on its summit whilst its base lay on the Equator.

A little later Mount Kenya had been sighted and by the early 1950's there was evidence that Ptolomy's map may have had some validity. Arab slave and ivory traders returning into Zanzibar from the deep interior had spoken of two huge lakes, one the Ujijy, the other the Myanza. As to whether these lakes were one, and at the same time the Source of the Nile, remained a mystery. Likewise, it was conjectured as to whether Mount Kilimanjaro and Mount Kenya were in fact the famed mountains of the moon. With such ambiguity and uncertainty the great age of central African exploration began. Richard Francis Burton and John Hanning Speke set off for Africa in 1856 eventually striking westward from Zanzibar and into an area no white man had entered before.

show off in front of the girls, and as ever Abdul came to take my order, moving his weary limbs from memory, a body press-studded together.

Terry was immersed in his Guardian Weekly, the only thing that stopped him talking. Maps and books from the University and British Council were piled high on the table. ''Cafe thsir or thee?'' Abdul's voice synchronised well with his mouth this morning, there was usually a fractional time delay. By the time his jaw had left its position adjacent to his nose to descend to talking position the sound was already leaking out, pursed lips puckered trying to catch up with the sounds. With characters like Abdul, if ever I wrote a book I decided I'd put in the introduction, 'All characters in this book exist, any resemblance to the original characters, however slight, is intentional'. He headed back to the kitchen using tables as landmarks, if one had been moved he stood a fair chance of ending up in the restaurant muttering and cursing.

The maps that I had bothered to bring with me, and there were two, were spread out on the table somewhere between croissants and Terry. Rumours were filtering through from overland travellers that the Turkana in North West Kenya were ambushing vehicles; the Turkana hadn't got any food. So, too, the recent closure of the Kenyan Tanzanian border would prevent my reaching southern Lake Victoria, Mwanza, which suggested I consider Zaire from South West Sudan, along the Juba-Yei road in the direction of Kisangani, formerly Stanleyville. Visas for Zaire, however, were presently difficult to get hold of and in any case the rainy season would make the roads impassable. This left one alternative, Uganda.

There was a legitimized fascination in entering a war zone, a

pathological glamour where one would absorb an optimism that no violence could unconvince, or a cynicism that would gnaw into the heart, mind or itself; malignant, hungry, belching out the lurid possibilities and the possible Elysian ascension. Perhaps my journey would now become a quest and the application of thought Quixotic. Pancho Villa chasing his master, a knight-errant confronting windmills on his way to La Mancha.

Diary

The thrill of this adventure is very intense and now I've decided to go all the way, there really is no turning back. I've tended to be so dismissive about my travels but I'm sure this trip will create some understanding back home of my motives. How can they refuse to acknowledge me and the experience I'm accumulating as a facet of communication?

Back at the hotel I sat on my bed as Mohammed stood by the window procrastinating. He reminded me of a cross between Frankie Howerd and Jimmy Clitheroe; a man with a slightly effeminate pose struggling with puberty. Splaying his feet, hand on hips, he would always hold his cigarette in a holder. Dorothy Parker without any wit. ''You know what I think,'' he would say, telling no one in particular, knowing everyone would hear, ''That Currie, he's a crazy man, the craziest man I ever knew''. Currie was a very dark coloured African Iraqui living in Kuwait. Like so many travellers he didn't know why he was here; like so many travellers he didn't always know where he was, but during the day he occupied the fourth bed. Currie was a boxer and once ran 10.3 for a hundred metres as Kuwaiti champion. He could have

Early morning papers in downtown Cairo.

squeezed Mohammed into a box one foot cube if he'd wanted to. Mohammed was a wimp. At night he roamed around the hotel with desultory insomnia, pausing to make tea or shower while everybody was asleep. Sometimes I would chat with him in the early hours. "Mohammed he very stupid man," Currie would say, breaking into a grin, "I'm a business man I'm a gentleman", mocking Mohammed's self-appraisal, "What's he doin' here then?" And that's all he ever had to say about life, the dissection of Mohammed piecemeal.

Then in the traveller's world no one really cared who you were; it's an egoistic preoccupation with the survival instinct, insupportably intact, palpable gestures. You're either one of us or you're not. When Currie did eventually sleep, Mohammed would invite new inmates into the hotel to view his half-open mouth, "See my friend Currie", he would sneer, dropping in a peanut so everyone could watch him cough.

The following morning, my twenty-fourth in Cairo, I made my fourteenth visit to the Sudanese Embassy, still trying to get my papers in order, still expecting the usual diffident reply. A book listing all the fortunate (or unfortunate) travellers having been granted permission to travel in Sudan was on display between 10am and midday, each day. A queue of cosmopolitan back-packers feverishly hoped today was their day; some hadn't got a back-pack, some hadn't got a hope. Perhaps twenty or more itinerant evergreens milled around an irregular quadrilateral courtyard, a glory hole where each one wore the 'uniform'. The armless waistcoat and the red-striped grandad-collared cheesecloth shirt; the head-band, the hair and that happy stuck-on smile procured from the land of laid back living. A land of paraphrased gestures and plagiarised talk, plugged into Dylan, Country Joe and a head full of sunshine; California Gold. "We're all into peace and freedom man, I mean Time and Space," scheduled CND and Greenpeace forever, and as the word is passed on from soul to soul the Time/Space continuum rockets to the moon.

John was in the corner staring into a void; too much time, too much money, and yet too much to do. Now he'd nothing left but would carry on South regardless. Peasants would give him food he said and he was right, they would. Such is the nature of simple living people without the contrived complexities of a fast hyped-up way of life. White skin is revered, and under the gaze of the moon and a packet of Rizzlas, that fatted calf would sure taste good. Beg your way through Sudan man for hark the fatted calf for all to see as little boys and girls blow out their bellies like balloons. The automatic process of hunger. The queue had gone and at the hatch the book at last showed me what I had been waiting for, now it was time to move on, and as I left someone grabbed my arm. "A little Bachsheesh, man, spread it around. Lost my passport, lost my money, everything, a little help ......" I turned around to see glazed eyes, a white boy and British. I turned away nauseated and left.

Within half an hour everything was packed. My toothbrush, swimming trunks and Bartholomew's map of Africa ...... there wasn't much. Blashfield-Snell would not have been impressed. Said goodbye to Terry, a moment more and I'd see glistening eyes behind metal-rimmed glasses and that is definitely not part of the game. 'Chow' all round, a quick glance and a smile and I was pedalling down Kasr el Nile across the tramlines past the bus station, Tahrir Bridge, the island, the second bridge. Then left on to Giza Road and the rotting grimy dusty suburbs with the bleating cars, blatant and loud and as fast as I could I pedalled, South towards upper Egypt, Luxor, Aswan and Sudan.

THE NILE VALLEY

On the Ning Nang Nong
Where the Cows go Bong!
And the Monkeys all say Boo!
There's a Nong Nang Ning
Where the trees go Ping!
And the tea pots Jibber Jabber Joo.

Spike Milligan.

The Valley had a two-lane tarmacadamed road all the way from Cairo to Aswan, a distance of 584 miles. It felt good to be 'on the road' again, wind blowing in my hair and the warm sun bronzing my arms and legs. Yet still I could smell Cairo, but shaking myself free with every turn of the pedals, at long last I was on my way.

The bike was moving well. I'd checked all the components before setting off, blown up the tyres and oiled the gears. I'd also washed off the grime of the city streets with a bowl full of Nile water, and young boys whistled and waved as I raced on by. The mass of labour, burnt-back farmers called fellahin, looked up with surprise — a surprise that smiled as they survived on the varying generosity of the river's annual flood and the constancy of their own unending field labours. I was starting to feel the threads weave together to form the beginning of an adventure, a series of which would culminate in the completion of a journey. Years of cycling enabled me to cover a hundred miles a day for ever if the roads were good, two hundred miles if I had to. I couldn't help wonder though how the Nubian Desert would affect the journey, it was only a week away and then what?

It took five days to reach Aswan, past El Minya, Asyut, across the river at Naq Hammadi, Luxor with the Valley of the Kings, and the wind was behind me all the way. And all the way I followed the railway line snaking beside the River Nile which was like a blue ribbon in a delicate green tapestry framed by a sand plateau. And at length, after five days riding, I was in sight of Aswan, far in the distance, wavering in the heat of the day.

I was dusty and hot and the Coke and Chia shop was a mirage by the harbour, with Sport Cola from Canada Dry served by a rather podgy Errol Flynn with his straight sophisticated hair falling gently over his forehead. A group of travellers sat around one of the tables and I ordered a drink. With a deft flick the bottle top burst from the neck with a whoosh and hit the roof before landing on someone's head. It was like an air gun at a fairground. He did this all day long and instead of a delicate sssch as when one conceals a movement it was a rap on the roof as subtle as the sound of breaking glass. My astonishment showed and he smiled without looking at me, if he'd aimed it properly he could have killed me, such was the force of the gas and such would be the final ignominy of such a death. ''Come and sit down man, you look absolutely bedazzled.'' I was and turned towards this lilting Irish voice; ''Here man, put yer bike over there and have my chair, you look as if you're doin' a good crack on that machine''. With genuine travellers one is absorbed and assimilated immediately for there is only one basic direction and they assumed I'd be going their way. ''The name's Seamus and this is the gang.'' He looked at me wryly and laughed at the motley crew, not unkindly.

A group of new people to meet, all drinking tea. Conversation stopped to acknowledge my presence and a long blonde-haired fellow turned towards me; "Do you know I've been a weck, all week". He looked haggered, stubbly and a little spotty. "I sit and sit and sit and when I stop sitting I'm shitting and I am wunning to the toiwet and I have had quite enough." He couldn't pronounce his b's, r's or his l's and coupled with a slight lisp and his beads, bangles and baggy-baggy trousers he was pathetic and I liked him.

A Dutchman called Bart sat next to a Swiss fellow, Ivan; there was a Scottish boy, two English lads — one from Liverpool, and with his back to me an American, one of the few that had ventured beyond Europe. "You're only just in time man, we'll be just going to the boat now, it'll be sure to be on its way," and at that everyone around got up and started walking towards the Port. Not, however, before I noticed a black African, probably Tanzanian, walking up to Errol to hand himself a Coke. Biting off the top with his teeth he drank the contents, handed back the bottle and looked at the bottle man with intent, leered and walked to follow us. If nothing else he had style.

With the nicest ideology in the world and in the finest tradition of travel, the boat was a shambles. Two double-tiered barges strapped at each side of a wreck. A grey-beard of a boat, a dugout, hoary-headed moribund and rheumy-eyed; the engine eased this decrepit tumbledown forward, smoke billowed from the funnel whilst floorboards decomposed, visibly growing moss in nooks and crannies. "Tis a wonderful life this travelling you know Nick," Seamus was the only one talking as we sat in a circle press-ganged to the fore of one of the barges. The boat, now gorged and replete, was infested with people. "Yes it is indeed it is, 'tis a wunderful, wunderful life I say Nick," said Seamus. "I say it beats working for a living. A little grape picking here and oranges there, tractor driving when I can get it. To think I spent all those years in London when I could have had this." And in a plain speaking sort of way I suppose he was right.

I imagined the Northern Line from Edgeware to Tottenham Court Road jam-packed with commuters, or the 125 bus along Hyde Road to Manchester Piccadilly, and yet travelling doesn't come easy. The monsoon rains in Sumatra pounded, there were no sun domes in that jungle. There were the bandits in Kashmir, concussion in the Himalayas and altitude sickness in the Rockies. And then the exhaustion, fatigue, the cramps, hunger, and the loneliness. Such terrible feelings of abstraction, a home-and-away alienation, never here but there, a recondite existence, monadic, a primary organic unit, a life with the valency of one.

"Fiwst impwessions are so bweutifool, no wot or pove'ty in this wake, so bwissfoo," said the German hippie. He stood up, surveying the 'wushing waters' as we groaned ahead, his orange and white pyjama trousers flapping around spindly legs. Check shirt unbuttoned inside a waistcoat, Bermuda sunscape printed on the back, blue cloth band wrapped round his head. "I once met a Dinka in Hamburg," he said, "A gweat big man, fwom the Dinka twibe you know, a bus dwiver. Wanted to change his name fwom John to Montazuma or something, Hamburg, can you imagine." I couldn't help but laugh at this affable skeleton of a man, his earrings chinked and he asked me why I was laughing, and I was, heartily, "How stwange", he said and looked again to his 'wippling waters'.

The journey to Wadi Halfa would take two days and two nights, non-stop unless the boat broke down and frequently it does. Food was bread and goat's cheese, bananas and dates, shared around. Seamus had a plastic box of halfa, a dry brittle crumbly sweetcake and one of the English lads made up a salad. The engines pumped away and the odd voice could be heard to stir as the moon rose against a swarthy black sky. This moon was different from the smog bound one in Cairo; the sluttiness had gone, more curvaceous now and bonny, primped to pretty-pretty. Perhaps it was the clear clean air which during the day lacerated the ground with shadows possessing the acuity of a carpenter's chisel. At night, long distance telescoped out of perspective and as the moon lay on the horizon, unblemished soft and full, with a little imagination one could moor alongside and climb to the top of a crater.

Next morning we breakfasted on the remains of the food bought in Aswan which would have to suffice until Wadi Halfa. I'd made a water bucket out of a jam can, hauling up lake water with a length of string. I suppose I should have used water purification tablets as hepatitis and cholera are endemic in Africa. And as I sat back sipping cool River Nile, life seemed very easy and pleasant.

When it comes to travelling it isn't a question of money because most places in the world can be visited with very little, it's really a question of approach. As ever the jingle 'it's not what you do but the way that you do it', is as apt sailing down the Nile as it is backpacking to Kathmandu. The American was a Nile cruiser and definitely on the wrong boat, "I've said this before and I'll say it again, this boat is a dump". It was "But fiwst impwessions are so bweutifool, quite quite wefweshing". Compared to the pseudo-sophistry of the Californian drawl, the German's mispronunciation appeared so congruous, pleasantly childlike in a world complicated with perfection.

The American would return to San Francisco with a becalmed glazed look in his eye; it is expected of him to have discovered his innermost self and return enlightened for all to see. The problem was his outer self couldn't cope with the scene; frustration and exasperation eeked out of his every gesture and glance, "Why, these goddam people don't know anything. I was talking to that man over there and he'd never heard of existentialism, can you imagine ...... " I'd so like the German to say that word, he'd give it far more meaning. "They're stupid, stupid people, how can I possibly make a film of this place if they don't communicate ......" The American had been a war photographer in Vietnam, or so he claimed, and suffered the presence of lesser beings with the assumption that napalm made a man of you and that camphor smoke in the nostrils was the only way of testing one's virility.

Now he was a film director/writer/actor and had a Bolex 16 mm camera that was only twenty-five years old; when it worked it sounded like a tumble drier. "I want to capture the debris of life,

you know what I mean, the beauty of poverty,'' and he went off to film another woman suckling her young when she had nothing left to give.

Putrescence and defilement are everywhere; you only have to look a hair's breadth beneath the surface, but that's only part of the story. 'Put on your make-up man, and dance a jig', said the film director, 'this will be a real scoop Harry', he whispered to his assistant, 'another unknown tribe ......'

The morning of the second day, it was rumoured, would give us a glimpse of Abu Simbul, that huge edifice carved out of the very mountain itself to commemorate Ramses and his wife, Hather, in the guise of Nefertari. Travellers along Egypt would be welcomed by Hather in her disguise to be embraced by a great civilisation. However, those adventurers entering Africa would first have seen the imposing Colossi of Ramses, a proud spur to Egyptians, a warning of Egypt's might to any fractious Nubians.

There was a commotion on the top deck. The monument drifted gently into view and the colossi towered in the distance. To revere a great artefact is almost a selfish appreciation. Under the moonlight alone one's sensations are gilded; to the chatter and ignorance of an accompanying crowd, less so. The American thought it was amazing, we didn't argue with him, but under the present conditions, over lunch, voted it a vulgarity.

The lads had largely drifted to sleep in the fresh breeze, cool in the shade. I felt surprisingly alert. Wadi Halfa could only be a few hours away, the lake was narrowing and people were slowly gathering their possessions. After Wadi Halfa, what then? Certainly not the comfort of people as the Nubian Desert would, the odd railway station apart, be lifeless. Moreover I was worried about the wind. It was difficult to ascertain in which direction it was blowing as the boat created its own artificial blend. Most of the time the wind blows due south and this had assisted me so far, an about-turn now would make the crossing too hazardous. Previous journeys on soft surfaces had taught me to ride hard and swiftly without stopping; once stopped it's not easy to continue and effort is at a premium.

As ever, pandemonium set in as the boat came within sight of a miniscular jetty. African pandemonium. Be it Asiatic, Arabic, Hellenistic or poor man's moody blues, the composure of rational man becomes a seething mass given the right conditions. A woman grabs her young, one under her arm, and one strapped to her back with a suitcase balanced on her head. Woven baskets, crammed with new stainless steel pots and pans, stand alongside red plastic buckets and yellow bowls strung together to be humped by little boys; bundles of rags are held in knotted sheets, rolls of carpets bend at each end. Then the boat eases into port, crunching to a halt, and everyone is hurled forward, particularly women, wares and baggage. The men carry stereo cassette radios, huge built-in speakers based on the premise that if it's big it's got to be good and if the music is loud so much the better.

The men walk off first and some hold hands, whilst the women gather in the scramble behind. Backpacks on, bikes loaded, we, the white contingent are hustled off among the chaos. Wadi Halfa harbour was a sandbank upon which squatted a handful of tin huts whose occupants sell basic dishes and tea twice a week, or whenever the boat bothers to arrive. Lorries and Toyota taxis tout for custom but within minutes the anarchy is over, and Seamus, Bert, Ivan and myself are left alone to tramp the last mile into town. This is Sudan.

twenty-two

Cleopatra

When I think of Egypt I visualise the pyramids. I see the River Nile and I imagine one of the most famous women of all, Cleopatra.

Cleopatra's voice has been immortalised in Rome by Greek biographer, Plutarh, as 'it was like an instrument of many strings', her beauty made perfect by Shakespeare in 'Anthony and Cleopatra' ''...... she did make defect perfection, and breathless, power breathe forth,'' and her commercial possibility by Julius Caesar, Mark Anthony and numerous eating houses in Cairo, all claiming to be the original 'Cleopatra Restaurant'.

She has come to represent, as no other woman of antiquity has, the prototype of the romantic femme fatale, and in the streets of Cairo, El Minya, Luxor and Aswan we can see the elongated beauty of Egyptian women with surely the most beautiful eyes in the world.

Cleopatra was born in 69BC, the second daughter of King Ptolemy XII and was destined to become the last sovereign of the Macedonian dynasty that ruled Egypt between the death of Alexander the Great in 323BC and its annexation by Rome

Subsequently they fell out and a civil war ensued, to which Julius Caesar intervened. Devastated by her charms he defeated all anti-Cleopatra opposition and placed her back in power with her husband/brother.

In 44BC Caesar was murdered by Brutus and after Caesar's unforeseen decline and fall, Mark Anthony became the heir-general of Caesar's empire; Octavius Caesar, nephew and personal heir was still a sickly boy. Anthony immediately sent for Cleopatra who was delighted because now she could pursue her ascent to power.

Cleopatra had first met Anthony when she was fourteen; now at twenty-eight she was well aware of her powers and set out to captivate the raffish and unstable ruler of the Roman Empire. Forgetting his wife, Fulvia, in Rome, he returned as Cleopatra's slave to Alexandria, where he treated her not as a protected sovereign but as an independent monarch. Living a life of debauchery and folly he eventually had to return to Italy to sort out his affairs. Fulvia had died so it was particularly prudent to marry

seduce Herod of Judea, one of the richest 'client kings' of Rome; this rebuff she greatly resented.

After the winter of 32-31 amidst great revelry in Greece, Rome finally declared war against Cleopatra and Anthony was relieved of all positions of power. At the naval Battle of Actium, in which Octavius faced the combined forces of Anthony and Cleopatra on 2nd September, 31BC, Cleopatra suddenly broke off the engagement and set course for Egypt. Inevitably defeat followed.

Cleopatra had to all intent and purposes made a complete mess of everything. She had backed two losers so all that she could hope for was undying renown. Inducing Anthony to kill himself for her would do just that and she retired to her mausoleum sending messages to her lover that she was dead. He fell on his sword only to botch it, so in a last excess of devotion or gross instance of incompetence, had carried himself to Cleopatra's retreat to find that she was in fact alive, and he died. How galling.

Rather than be dragged amidst

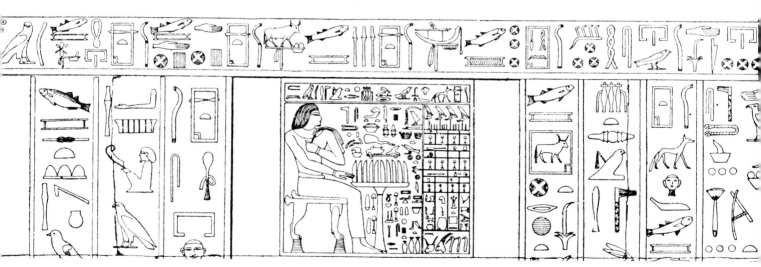

in 31BC. Cleopatra, from her Greek descent had no Egyptian blood, but for political reasons regarded herself as the daughter of Re, the sun god. Her beauty was such that while Plato ordinarily admitted to four sorts of flattery, Cleopatra, he said 'had a thousand!' When Cleopatra's father died his son took over, marrying his sister Cleopatra for good measure.

Octavius's sister, Octavia. Then he went East again to ask Cleopatra for money to carry out his postponed Parthian campaign and ended up marrying her. This insulted Octavia and her brother but in Roman law it was invalid and all Rome became united against him.

Cleopatra's greed was to be her undoing and whilst Anthony was away she tried unsuccessfully to

the shouting variety of Rome and 'amidst slaves with greasy aprons' she applied a poisonous asp to her bosom to become, as the legend goes, united with her Anthony.

And as I cycle along the Nile Valley I can think of one quote from Mae West, in 'I'm No Angel', that has a great romantic feel;

''Beulah, peel me a grape''!

If there had been sufficient cars to fill a large space, Wadi Halfa wouldn't have been a town but a car park. The most impressive components of this lunik settlement were the central square and the wind, notably because there was nothing else there. A veritable sea of tranquillity.

The lake bordered the north as did the railway to the east, the market to the west and the actual town south. Within such confines this near half mile square of nothingness all but absorbed three rusting tin huts bending with the wind. On the edge of the square stood a brightly coloured metal box with painted clouds appealing to fantasy; red, yellow, green and blue with Pepsi-Cola daubed in black shaky script. When the generator was working, with the express purpose of serving ice cold fruity-fresh lemonade, the wind carried the noise of the thumping motion for miles. Across the square, large rubber-wheeled trailers dragged, harnessed behind well-groomed horses; either empty or full but never half so. The only time anyone would sit in the square was after sunset and that coincided with the only time the wind wheezed and slowed down. This was the time to eat and drink, to bow down in prayer and to think awhile with a little haphazard conversation to punctuate a hard day's work.

The wind was quite against me, blowing north, and a decision had to be made as to whether I could cross the Nubian. With mid-day temperatures soaring above 48°C I couldn't risk a head wind; the rate of body evaporation would be too rapid and I wouldn't be able to carry sufficient water to survive. So, too, at slow speeds the sand would skewer the front wheel to the right or left to skate the bike out of balance. The effort needed to overcome the inertia of the bike through an inch or two of sand is greater than that needed merely to continue, and with a wind so forceful I wouldn't be able to obtain the optimum speed. With all the freedom inherent in adventure there are always governing factors which regulate and control.

Each morning around 5am I checked the wind direction; still it was blowing the wrong way, so still I had to wait. I'd wake Bart, the Dutchman, and he'd wake the Swiss fellow Ivan to breakfast and drink tea in any one of several 'chai-shops' in the market. By 11am it was time for elevenses at the fish shop on what any other small town would call the High Street. Each morning the head would be chopped off a huge Nile perch and a greasy hackman from Hades would split the belly from head to tail. With a bagful of garlic and sliced lemon we would wait for the first batch of chopped-up fish to emerge from the filthy scum-ridden-offal-laden-festering-flyborn wok cooking over a kitchen fire. Everything was dirty.

"He's mad you know, don't talk to him," a voice whispered across the table. "Don't talk to him, he's mad, very, very mad. Sssch he's mad." The voice popped out of an unshaven old man with a hobble and three warts on the top of his nose. "They say I'm mad but I'm not. He's madder than me, a lot madder than me I can assure you," and this funny little fellow with a few hairs sticking out of his head got up to leave. "You'll see, you'll see, you'll see." He gargled a glass of water, spat it out and hobbled into the street chuckling as a group of lads in the corner sniggered.

The fish shop had four long benches each seating ten hungry people and long wooden tables from which to eat. 10am - 12 noon was peak service time and always full. A granite giant of a man sat opposite me; he was big, very black and stared at me intently. "What's your name?" He directed his question like a car exhaust backfiring. A man in the far corner shook his head as if to warn me and apart from the sizzling pan all was quiet. "What's your name first?" I said, hoping my fish wouldn't arrive yet as I suddenly didn't feel very hungry. He looked at me in a very raw manner, perplexed and his left eyebrow started to twitch as if the simplest of questions pushed him into circuit overload, steam pouring out of his overheated head. He leaned forward, elbowing his way towards me, struggling vainly with his twitching left eyebrow. A pause. "My name is Mister Kitchen Table ...... what is your name?" "Oh Mister Wooden Chair," I said with inspiration, then immediately regretted my boldness in front of a crowd as I contemplated a lowdown nervous breakdown. I had visions of his spade-like hands gripping me around the throat to immerse me headfirst into the wok. His rubber lips pursed and his eyes honed in on me restricting all peripheral information. I didn't know whether to laugh or to run, be assertive or shrivel. "Hah ... hah ... hah." Everyone not quiet went quieter as he stood up, laughing like a donkey in pain. "Hah ... hah ... hah ... Mister Wooden Chair ... very, very good, very good ... Mister Wooden Chair, yes I see it now ......" and he heavy-stepped his way on to the street, half maniac half man, half shouting Mister Wooden Chair and I sat back, trembling, as the fish arrived crisp, hot and tender.

Again and again I'd looked south only to feel the wind blowing in my face. Habub sand storms could be seen in the dust-darkened sky far out on the horizon, and scaled down tornadoes whisked across the square. Men crouched low, hanging on to their skull caps, and small children ran away yelping. On such occasions I climbed to the top of the rocky buttress which was directly behind the rest-house. Fragments of mountain ricocheted to the valley plain as I climbed up high and stood five hundred feet above the town, head bent, face covered towards the south and the wind.

The wind died down as quickly as it rose and as the sun set the plaintive cry of the Muezzin drifted airily to a people in prayer. Up here the town looked so small, Lego shops and a Hornby station littered with a handful of wagons. Microdot people walked across the square, some holding hands, and when the wind allowed snatches of conversation could be heard. The odd dog barked, and occasionally a car engine would cough, but that was all.

I was staying in a small open-air rest house on the edge of the market square, which was also the edge of the desert. At night a breeze would filter into the clay-packed courtyard, natural ventilation sweeping away the tight night heat. Each bed was a wooden frame on legs with a string/hessian binding interlaced as a mattress. The joints were crudely made and the pegs holding them together would be loose, making every movement wooden and the darkness became a creaky night. Half the courtyard was covered with hundreds of thatched bundles tied together and laid across a fretwork of slender palm branches joined to square connecting beams of African mahogany. During the day the shade would give some respite from the heat but at night I lay under the stars with my cotton sleeping bag wafting and once almost indiscernibly I heard the beating of drums far away in the distance.

The American was sitting in a chai shop by the station waiting for the twice a week morning train to leave for Khartoum. I strolled over to say hello; Bart and Ivan tagged along. He was absorbed in his own conversation, "I'm doing this spiritual journey. I've been an actor, film-maker, writer and now I want to make a film." The fellow he was talking to was a teacher of the Koran and said little as a group of men clustered around paying token appreciation. "I'd call the film 'Bahai versus Islam'. Well Islam is the final religion, of course, but that's why we have wars." He started to pound gently on his knees, "I say my religion is best, you say yours. This is my theory; Islam, Christianity, Hinduism, you name it they all have their holy wars", and he banged his knees harder to demonstrate his argument. "My religion is best, my religion is best, my religion is best ......" The dust kicked about his agitated feet and the group of tea swillers gathered to form a crowd. The teacher, a youngish cleanly-dressed fellow started to speak. "My friend you must accept certain conditions when you enter a country that isn't your own; go along with their way of life, respect their customs, the way they think and the way they are." The American stood up, leaning on his walking stick, "Hell, this is hell. I've been brutalised in Sudan; no running water, no sanitation, the food's disgusting and the drinking water is black".

The American was a little hysterical, his face taut and empty, his spiritual journey was wearing thin today. His walking stick fell to the ground along with his pocket telescope, his Swiss army knife and his khaki canvas hat; he was nearly in tears and I felt very sorry for him. The teacher continued "I'll be going to the Nubian mountains for several days to study, taking nothing but a little water; you must relax my friend, relax and enjoy life, you have to because you're a long way from home." Then he got up and eased his way through the crowd. The American hung low muttering deeply and continued to wait for the train, wishing with all his heart it would come now and take him far away. But there would be no place of rest for this man in Sudan, no respite from Africa because Africa is Africa and not the concept the West attaches to it with all the false assumptions and values we place there, and the American was face to face with his adversary; he was going to lose and he knew it.

Ivan brought three teas as Bart and I sat on the ground, resting against the side of a small mud-hardened wall. Bart was a very sensible-looking traveller, maybe it was his glasses or maybe his well-cut trousers but he'd had a lot of crazy days in down-town Amsterdam. Sudan for him was the return to a simpler more natural way of life, swopping 'sixties psychedelia for the 'eighties brand of realism.

Difficulties arise on a journey however, usually during the transition from 'knowing' to 'being'. 'Knowing' something is so is not the same as it 'being' so; one might be true whilst the other is completely so. Smiling faces tell me I'm surrounded by friends and when they put their arm around me, laugh, joke and while away very pleasant hours, I know it's true; but it's not. The actual 'Being' on a journey is the exploitation of the traveller. Travelling is not a process of enhancement but one of coping with humility, for he is not and never will be 'at one' with the people he passes.

This is Threadbare Street in Cinderella city and I am one of the Governors of a faraway plutocracy where land is a life of milk and honey. With a return ticket to El Dorado in my pocket, the wealth differential between them and myself was too great for either side to fully understand and the implications of such discrepancies in life too hard to accept. I would never know what it would be like to live a day-to-day hand-to-mouth existence where thoughts for the future rarely recognised more than two or three months ahead. And they, meaning that abstract being on the Nubian desert, would not know that within my own candied existence there lingered occasionally the fragrance of absinthe, the bitter principle of wormwood. My own oscillation between what I know I can do and what I won't be allowed to. Between the fluttering of butterfly wings and the butterfly catcher mounting his specimen in a cleanly polished glass case.

Sipping tea, the three of us knew another stage of the journey was near; they would get on the train with the American and I'd wait for the wind to change. I sensed any day my own journey commencing; the waiting had only served to excite me more, and filled me with apprehension. Brown walls nearby baked evenly in the heat as the air simmered. Whispery air, thin and fine drifted upwards into the hazy blue of an ocean becalmed. The edges of the walls were sharply defined, brown clay against blue sky and as I stared, the wall was quite quite still except for the very tiniest of wavers in the midst of oven-blown air; and for that instant, that totally secluded isolated moment, this strong and solid brown wall and the vaporous transient air were one and the same, both drifting along the plain, shimmering.

By evening everyone had gone and I was the only traveller left in the whole of North Sudan. Alone that is until the next boat pulled into port and two or three young hopefuls would begin their very own adventure on a hard-packed well-worn trail. I certainly wouldn't be there to meet them. The wind was still, which I was told would favour me by morning so I packed my few possessions into my panniers, ready.

Dawn varies here by a few minutes only throughout the year, and having to spend a week in Wadi Halfa I knew immediately the wind was blowing south, strongly. Rising I wrapped up my sleeping bag and before wheeling the bike silently out of the rest-house checked my water bottle. For provisions I had dried dates, bananas, boiled eggs, a large piece of dried fish and two loaves of bread. Over the square I rode towards the railway line. Palms waved, the only town furniture that had any movement, it was even too early for donkeys to bray. A quick glance behind, onto the sand-covered sleepers between the track lines and a hard push to overcome the dreaded inertia. A little speed, the wind now behind me, past the sleeping town on my right, forever south, south across the Nubian desert.

THE NUBIAN DESERT

You know son, I sit here in the pub drinking my pint listening
quietly to the people around me and their casual conversation
and I can't help but think that there's more substance in
dreams.

Dad.

The Nubian crossing, far from being a great feat was in my reckoning going to be no more than another isolated façet of a larger lonely whole. I respected the Nubian desert no more and no less than any other aspect of each of my previous journeys. The Sinai between Ismailia and Neot Sinai had a good road but it was long and sparse. The North West Thar desert on the Rajasthan Plain between Bombay and Delhi was also long, one thousand miles, and an April summer wind to stupefy those who dare to cross it — shrivelling possibilities and dessicating everything. So too the Deccan Plateau. I was without water for nearly three days; an Indian wilderness between villages and the Mojave in Arizona made me nauseous by day and delirious at night. The Nubian Desert was one of the hottest in the world but still I didn't entertain any notion of great endeavour.

Naturally I took precautions, researched the route reasonably well and prepared myself physically, but adventure had transcended reason. Perhaps this is a great danger, perhaps reason never had any part in adventure. The simple straightforward fact was that I no longer conceded the possiblility of failure. To admit to the possibility is to enter into a cause and effect situation, the thought of failure precipitates it happening. This doesn't mean to say that I wasn't aware of the difficulties, but hardships are relative and for me the Nubian would be hard and hot, spiced with solitude but nothing more. That's because it is nothing more, maybe something less.

With the best possible intentions I would try to elaborate on the possibility of a desert crossing, which is blatantly absurd. For most people it would be absurd as a feasible consideration to seriously embark on such a project, but then I wouldn't be able to climb Everest with ease and Mesner or Bonnington wouldn't easily be able to do as I. It seemed so out of context to examine what cannot be accomplished when that consideration has been discarded.

I'd covered forty miles that first morning after leaving Wadi Halfa, riding on the sleepers between the tracks which had long since been covered by howling Habub sandstorms giving a dusty firm surface. Apart from the occasional Jebel (hill), the land lay quite flat to stretch the horizon as far as it would go. The wind, such that it was, blew behind me and progress was fairly good as the sand remained firm enough to cycle.

By what I thought to be mid-day I rested for a while, sitting against a telegraph pole. If there had been a rock in view I would have fought hard for the privilege to have a moment's shade, but this land on the edge of time itself had all its rocks atomised long ago so that not a single mountain or monument existed any larger than the size of a stone. The sun bore down and instantly evaporated any sudden movement; I reached for a boiled egg, a few dates and my water bottle. The water was hot and tasted of rusting metal, piped muddily from the Nile. I had a little over a gallon to last me to the first known water hole at the hundred and twenty mile mark, just under two day's ride from Wadi Halfa.

Diary

The desert appears lifeless and empty. Seen no-one and heard nothing, not even the wind. I can't help wondering what would happen if the bike collapsed or for that matter if I did. It will be four days until a train passes, if it turns up at all, and there's nowhere to hide from the sun. I suppose I'll survive but the thought that I might not doesn't worry me unduly ......

The Camel

The camel probably deserves first mention amongst animals that have successfully adapted to the desert and for most people this animal is the very symbol of survival in a barren land.

One hump or two! Well, both species belong to the same genus, Camelus. The Bactarian camel had two humps and the Dromedary has one, existing only in Asia. The only one-humped camels known today are purely domesticated animals, their wild ancestors in Mesopotamia [3000 BC] are now extinct. The one-humped camel reached Egypt from Mesopotamia about four thousand years ago, spreading into the Sahara and the Nubian Desert probably only a few decades before the beginning of the Christian era.

The camel really is a marvel of the desert as every feature of the animal is contrived to assure survival in a hot climate. If you look at a camel from a distance there are three characteristics that can immediately be seen; firstly the long legs, secondly the large body with hump or humps, and thirdly, the long neck.

The long legs give the camel its running speed and endurance, it being important wherever possible to escape its enemies swiftly. At least that was true in the past, now it has no natural enemies.

As the Sahara is becoming sparser, and the Nubian desert is on the edge of the Sahara, camels must cover longer distances to reach food, hence the endurance of the legs. The long legs serve yet another purpose. In the summer a layer of hot air forms just above the

ground and ends at about the level of the underside of the adult camel's body. The vital organs are therefore kept marginally cooler being situated in a slightly cooler layer of air. The camel's dinner-plate sized feet act as would snow-shoes, preventing it sinking in soft sand, the weight spread over a greater surface area. It has been suggested that people of some nomadic tribes in the desert have larger and broader feet than Europeans. I take size sevens.

Secondly, warm-blooded animals who live in temperate or warm climatic zones maintain a constant temperature gradient between the warm body and the cooler environment. In the desert the temperature of the air is higher than that of the camel's and if this high temperature were to be transmitted to the camel's body, it would die.

From above the camel has the shape of a camera lens on its side and the perpendicular rays of the sun are kept away from the bulk of its body. So too, unlike animals in cooler climates, the camel hasn't got an evenly distributed layer of fat around its body, it's all in the hump. And because uninsulated body tissues can radiate away body heat more easily, heat is dispersed that much more efficiently.

The hump, in actual fact, is not filled with water as was long thought, but fat. The camel can drink up to 250 pints of water when parched, in ten minutes. The water is then temporarily stored in the stomach which has a capacity for 525 pints. Subsequently it is

evenly distributed throughout the animal's tissues and also the red blood corpuscles which can expand to 240 times their original volume.

Every vital process, however, is dependent on a constant input of energy and in order to create energy by the metabolic process, living organisms must take in nourishment often. As the camel feeds on camel's thorns, a bush with prickly shoots and leaves containing a good deal of water, the fat is built up in the hump and each hump can weigh up to thirty pounds. As the hump grows, some of the water drunk is chemicaly bound into the fat and stored thus. During the metabolism of the stored fat, hydrogen is produced which unites with oxygen in respiration to form water. When half a pound of fat is burned about a pint of water is produced and up to thirty per cent of the camel's body weight can be lost.

When summer temperatures rise to over 50°C [122°F] in the shade, the camel can no longer radiate body heat so it switches on to a further characteristic which is thought to be unique amongst mammals and birds. The camel can withstand an increase in the temperature of its body, and blood, of 8°C [16°F] above normal.

The third characteristic of the camel consists of the head and the tip of the hump. As mentioned already, the hump protects the body from the sun's rays, but the head perched on a long neck reaches above the probable upper limit of most sandstorms, so allowing the camel to breathe air relatively free of sand.

thirty-seven

[Previous page]

"Deserts offer the most naked conditions available to nature for which only the barest framework exists on which to hang tangible thoughts and I'd think the craziest ideas. Ideas that can only be rationalised under such stripped conditions catalyzed by active ingredients within the cosmos, like perfume on a beautiful woman, persuasive only as long as she is close ......"

As the sun produced long shadows from my right I'd covered another thirty-five miles, all day climbing the long, low rise. Making camp was simply a matter of laying out my sleeping bag. I ached terribly and the tops of my arms were badly burnt but the first day was over, as I lay engulfed in blackness; the swarthiness of Nubian night was like the inside of a womb with the moon just about to rise.

Deserts offer the most naked conditions available to nature for which only the barest framework exists on which to hang tangible thoughts and I'd think the craziest ideas. Ideas that can only be rationalised under such stripped conditions catalysed by active ingredients within the Cosmos, like perfume on a beautiful woman persuasive only as long as she is close, scents from the stars. Here I was a captive audience forced to look at the stars and attempt pitifully to make some comparison with their existence and my own.

How often I have asked myself why it was necessary to search for something so intangible that it might not exist. To prove to myself in an impersonal world the need for something other than total rigid conformity and that everyone has a right to some kind of immortality, some kind of unique self-esteem not couched with terms of bravery or courage. It's almost as if one becomes an object of observation to the 'other', the observer. To be written about and assessed, a prediction of behaviour. To become a commodity. So one reciprocates and likewise tries to reduce the observer to the status of a thing, such is the nonchalant amorality of the neutralist. Such also are the desert thoughts of an isolated mind, as insubstantial as a thumb-print in the sand, perhaps less so.

At that moment in time the present seemed only a part of a whole and though related to 'now' neglects the future. Who was it who said that "the parts of man are always in the future with his projected consciousness, and to that effect I am what I am and what I'm going to be, what I cannot be or do and what I could have done".

Watching the moon rise was like watching it sink, for it was bulbous and heavy with moon juice, hallucinating slightly so as to heave itself across the void. Whenever I looked up into the desert night the stars were always there, and later the moon. As a symbol the moon can be easily associated with isolated places because often it is the only object moving, the only sign of life a moving traveller can relate to and confide in.

In front of the moon on the desert plain one does not have to act. Like a waiter, an explorer's behaviour is essentially ritualistic. When the waiter bends forward in a manner which is too deeply expressive of concern and deference for the diners, the explorer explains and prepares his journey in minutae ad nauseum. When the waiter balances his tray in a manner which is just a little too precarious, the explorer introduces death-defying hazards that could kill him. Both waiter and explorer play with their condition in order to realise it, giving themselves no choice, wholly absorbed in their job.

As with the mime of the peculiar waiters' dance, there is too the extraordinary explorers' waltz, round and round; those who would row the Atlantic, accomplish North Pole crossings or cycle around the world must convey the desires of the onlooker who wishes to be able to think of that person as an explorer — different, strange, and eccentric. My mind wandered a little as I was drifting off to sleep, the telegraph wires hummed an airy harmony and far, far away I heard the faintest sound imaginable, so faint they couldn't really be heard and yet they were there; the drums beating, riding on the crest of a wave to the tune of a desert wind.

''By mid-day the sun burned; there was nowhere to hide and I had to rest for an hour sitting lazily on the railway line. Heat shimmering mirages flooded the wadis far away; I would have gone to fill up my water bottle but I still had the presence of mind not to go, in a desert one wonders how long presence of mind will last.''

By the time the sun had risen I'd been on the road for two hours, pushing the bike in twilight haze, dawn on my left, darkness on my right. The dates were finished, half the bananas had been eaten, as had most of the eggs. A little more problematic was the water, I had about four pints to last me until the next water hole, which was now about forty-five miles away. Most of the morning I managed to cycle, but deep sand across the track became more frequent, occasionally lasting several hundred yards. The wind was strongly behind me and in the near distance sandstorms raged across the celibate landscape forming a veil across pubescent ground, arresting beauty itself. By mid-day the sun burned; there was nowhere to hide and I had to rest for an hour sitting lazily on the railway line. Heat shimmering mirages flooded the wadis far away; I would have gone to fill up my water bottle but I still had the presence of mind not to go; in a desert one wonders how long presence of mind will last.

All the food was finished and I conserved a last pint of water. The water hole would be less than ten miles away, about one hours' journey, so I kept going and before long I saw a small square building lying in ruins. This was a spot marked 'X' on the map but the ill-fired clay bricks crumbled to the touch and the original red sheen was now brown. A well stood to one side. The winding mechanism was Victorian and obsolete, there hadn't been any water here for years. The heat was blistering and I sat down again slowly by the well wall. This had shaken my presence of mind far more than any mirage. The next water hole was at least forty miles away and I had nothing left to drink. I could die but all I thought of was Cairo.

It had taken me a long time to appreciate Cairo's finer points but I could see them clearly now. She remained a scarlet woman, ruthlessly diffident, with face powder flaking from well blushed cheeks, but she had all I wanted. Strawberry juices, orange or mango, banana freshly pressed through grated ice, bean fowl and pigeon or even roast chicken and chips. Country Joe would be strumming away and Crosby, Stills and Nash would be playing 'Marrakesh Express' in the record shop owned by Gerry the Greek next to the Rada Cinema where Roger Moore was playing Bond in 'For Your Eyes Only'.

So many things I wanted correlated with those I needed, whilst a white chested peregrine passively circled above me, my very own Fletcher seagull to haunt me, except this was a falcon. As it circled it drifted gently with the up-draught of rising hot air; I felt too tired to move on.

If I'd got on the train it wouldn't have meant that I'd failed, but that the heat of the sun and the isolation were simply factors in the situation which I chose to regard in a particular light, as a challenge to be enjoyed or as something I could no longer bear. I suppose failure is a part of freedom, to have the choice not to succeed; but everything is experience so it seemed to be simply a question of tolerance and the usefulness of acquiring such endeavour. As my little companion's feathers fluttered above, I had that choice but didn't want to carry it through to its logical supine conclusion.

Slowly it occurred to me that there are few if any birds in the Nubian desert, if fact very little life at all, and this little thing couldn't have flown far without a drink. I got up with great effort, sweat pouring from me, and my head throbbed in waves to fill me with nausea as I pedalled stiffly whilst the bird flew on ahead. I felt like the Mariner following the Albatross. Sure enough, after what seemed an eternity I climbed over the horizon to see people in the distance by round clay-baked turrets, and, wonders of all, a train.

Freewheeling into the station, I found a few hard-baked huts, which sold bean stew and tea, as passengers milled around the shade of a tree. The train had obviously just arrived, its red and yellow diesel engine looked hardy and the string of white carriages bore an elegant orange streak. I bought tea and several people offered me water which was cool, incredibly cool and sweet to a parched throat. The sudden infusion of liquid made me a little giddy and I sat down on the ground with a plate of rice cake in gravy and as ever, more tea.

Of course, everyone was talking to me, asking me obscenely stupid questions; maybe I'd ridden through a metropolis without noticing; how many towns were there between here and Wadi Halfa? I felt too glazed to talk and blatantly didn't. Immediately I sensed a divide, they thought I was crazy and I thought them parochial; unfair on both sides. The train hooted and moments later shunted forward as everyone scrambled aboard, instantly forgetting about me. I heard someone shout 'It's quicker by train', which sounded like an advert for British Rail; but whether it was stupid self-ruinous subjecticism or windy mysticism from too many beans, I knew I could cycle further than any train could take me, to go where trains don't go.

I bought some more dates, bananas and eggs; well stocked even for an emergency I also purchased an old plastic container, filled it with water and strapped it firmly onto the front pannier. As the train rolled out of sight so did I, not sorry to leave, to be alone again.

Refreshed and past the half-way point I was now going ever-so-slightly downhill. To think that Kitchener had inadvertently enabled me to cross the Nubian and had the good grace to make the railway long and straight. That afternoon I covered nearly fifty miles, which meant a final ride to Abu Hamed the following day of seventy miles. That would effectively mean I would be halfway between Wadi Halfa and Khartoum, and as a road of sorts continues through Berber and Atbara, I'd be there in three or four days' time. I was anxious to enter Central Sudan as the impending rainy season threatened to close the road to Juba.

Night fell once again and the air was still, the moon full and bright and in the distance far, far away someone was walking towards me, slowly. An eerie feeling crept down my spine as I lay in my sleeping bag, holding my breath as when I was a child, tense and silent.

I knew I'd have to face up to the possibility of meeting someone in abstract circumstances, never an easy meeting. I couldn't raise an arm or a leg and the man, that I could now recognise kept on walking, and at the same time he wasn't, simply getting closer. An impression of being near. The light was playing a trick or was it my imagination stapling me to the ground, preventing me from realising whether I was awake or asleep. Perhaps my imagination, the creator of everything, was giving my worn out mind something tangible to grip on to in this silent sound-proofed insulation chamber. I could hear in the darkness the murmur of madness decanting into the wind and I shivered a little unable to discover whether I was dreaming or not.

Diary

People walking backwards hand in hand, trees upside down and dogs turned into goats. The music deadens all exterior sound. A man walks towards me but I don't hear the sound of his footfall. He floats because I don't hear him walking and he appears now in slow motion. An occasional glance to create the feeling of movelessness, timelessness, nothinglessness, hopelessness. The void in the epicentre of a dream.

[Previous page] Water bearing children wave as I pass.

Aching with fatigue and shaking just a little, Abu Hamed appeared in the distance. It had taken me eighteen hours to do seventy miles, sand-drifts clogged the gears and I punctured five times. The ball bearings in the chain wheel bottom bracket crunched with grit and it was now dark, but the hardest part of the crossing was over. A night market was in progress, hurricane lanterns flickered and pressure pump-up lamps hissed incandescent light. Market stalls displayed bananas, eggs, and dates, as well as tomatoes, green peppers, coconuts; nothing I hadn't seen before. Chai ladies sat by their charcoaled stainless steel kettles, tea quietly brewing, steam trickling from the spout. Sweetened with honey and goat's milk, it tasted delicous and with a little goat's cheese wrapped in fresh oven-warmed bread I started to feel better. Locals chatted and were oblivious of my presence; obviously the train stopped here, so I wasn't the first traveller they had seen. The air was warm and everything felt good as I lay back against the tree putting my empty glass on the ground. I closed my eyes and a sense of relief and satisfaction impregnated my thoughts until they faded away, like a dog when he's tired who slept the moment he stood still.

The next two days passed quickly as the route was occasionally tarmaced. Atbara, a large bustling town, was a graveyard for steam engines. As I biked along the station there must have been a hundred rusty museum pieces falling apart. Further on, the hilly out-crops of Umah came into view, surrounded by trees and a long strip of cultivated greenery. Then the borderless graveyard on the outskirts of Shendi. A single acre of green crop stood alone amongst thousands of acres of arid land, then a military camp, buff coloured buildings with green shuttered windows. Little boys tried to sell me 'Gum-o' chewing gum, candy squared and neatly wrapped. Allotments of houses each with a wall and pastel-coloured metal gates enclosed in a garden, that sign of self-esteem for all to see. Finally Khartoum, the sprawling outskirts, the flat-looking city skyline, the traffic, the hum of people, 1,358 miles covered, with just under two thirds of the journey yet to go.

KHARTOUM TO SOUTHERN SUDAN

You imagine what you desire
You will what you imagine
You create what you will.

Invictus. William Ernest Henley.

The stillness of the desert around Khartoum was in perfect harmony with the silver light that was beginning to glow over the eastern horizon. The brilliant pattern of stars was extinguished as life began to return to the city and in the back streets steam rose into the cool air as tea-makers prepared for the arrival of the workers. Among the lush labakh trees lining the banks of the Blue Nile, birds twittered the moment they woke up and the angular sail of a felucca moved slowly along the river.

I'd been in Khartoum a couple of days and was staying in the youth hostel. The shower was incontinent and dripped non-stop into a rusty tin can appropriately placed to catch the residue water. Each of four dormitory rooms contained eight beds and if anywhere in town sheltered itinerant travellers, this was it.

Chris had cycled from Zimbabwe and was on his way to London. He'd climbed half way up Kilamanjaro and bore a full-sized rucksack on his specially-strengthened panniers. He was going to cross the Nubian by train and marvelled how I could exist carrying so little. Nigel was a free-living-bread-baking-theatre-workshop person who regularly supported the Campaign for Real Ale in Sheffield, his home town. After doing an agricultural degree he now wanted to know how potatoes should really be grown. 'The year of the potato is nigh,' he said and reckoned he'd backed a winner. I couldn't agree more.

Characters in Khartoum, a more unlikely place would be hard to find as Government officials often discarded three-piece suits for large white jellabias, emmas, and ebony walking sticks to give that little something which Western dress didn't have. Shops and offices opened around 8 o'clock in the morning only to close for breakfast at nine. After an hour's break everything creaks open, only to close again for the day at 2 o'clock and the streets of Khartoum again become silent and deserted.

Everyone I spoke to constantly invoked the name Allah in their conversation. Allah is thanked if things turn out well. (Allahamdu lillah); his approval is sought when plans are made or if tomorrow is mentioned (insh Allah — if God wills it) and to express aetheism is to incur utter disbelief. Two things that one doesn't do are to criticise Allah and flirt with Sudanese women. Whilst being a great pastime in the Western world, here it would bring down heavily the wrath of close male relatives in no uncertain terms. Nonetheless the delicate features of coffee-coloured cheekbones acted as a platform for that very rare but occasional occurence, a secret glance.

Each day I called into the Air France office to send a telex to Francesca in the New Bond Street Office — she promptly relayed the news to mum and dad. Each day I called in to see another friend of a friend, Mister Lussinian, the Armenian goldsmith, who was also an explorer. He thought my journey was impossible and all I wanted was a ride on the Blue Nile in his twin-engined Mercury-powered speedboat. When he finally took me out for a spin it felt like a day's holiday that I'd earned for crossing the Nubian and ripples reflected the crystallised pattern of the moon at speed. And as the sandflies blew in my face, I knew it was but a moment's relaxation before I began the next stage through Central Sudan to Juba.

The wind, as always, was directly behind me, almost allowing me to freewheel. The desert remnants within the city limits passed by to reveal a slim cultivated band of foliage; tea, sugar cane and puffy balls of cotton along the banks of the Blue Nile. I'd meet the White Nile again at Kosti and that would take me to her Source while the Blue Nile would veer off across Dinder to Ethiopia and the Choke Mountains, to Wallo and to Welega. After twenty-five miles cycling covered in the hour, I pulled off the road and made for a road-side tea shop situated on a raised patio covered by a corrugated roof held up with sky-blue poles. Life for the next two weeks at least would now revolve round cycling, feeding and sleeping.

Although being acclimatised to the heat I still found it difficult at midday and wherever I stopped several boys gathered around the bike asking the usual questions; where I was going and where I'd been, only to wave away the answers. It's all a question of courtesy. I ordered Cacadah, a dark red berry juice boiled and cooled, and the flies swarmed. Red Toyota pick-ups came and went, plush customised interiors with red velvet chairs and then a warm plate of beef was placed before me.

I allowed myself thirty minutes' maximum rest each time I stopped which was normally no more than four times a day. By nightfall I'd reached Kamlien for a final evening meal. Another time, another place, cafeteria Hafiz had singularly the most unappealing decor I had ever seen. Nile green pillars descended to bilious lime chairs, Chlorophyll plastic cups and waiters in green jellabias. Everything was green, even the neon which was the epitome of gaudy prettyism, giving the beef chunks a sickly hue.

After a night's noisy sleep one hundred metres into cotton balls and scrub, I wheeled myself back onto the main road and two hours later I stopped for breakfast at Haiseheish on the banks of the river. The market Souk comprised of two rows of corrugated tin huts placed parallel and if last night's cafe was grizzly green then life here shouted out in bag-pipe blue. A very loud man was screeching menus out of every food hatch out of every hut; plates of beef chunks skedaddled out in plastic bowls as a collapsed bagette was slapped hard beside. Breakfast always included an onion and tomato vinaigrette salad with gross bunches of asparagus leaves. A small plastic pot was divided into two halves, one side for salt, the other cayenne, so hot it tickled the throat first thing in the morning and pleasantly deadened the taste of the beef.

Souks are like fairgrounds, full of gunpowder, striped and colourful with a character on each corner and a different smell with every step you take. Have a coke and a smile, a jamboree milk shake, have a juice and a jive, the obligatory grease-backed hair leaving the scent of cow fat on the tips of your fingers.

On the banks of the river tens of men and young boys were bathing, handwashing their clothes, squatting as they pounded on rocks worn smooth. The breeze was fresh and within the morning I'd covered another sixty miles, one hundred in five hours so far. How strange it is that as soon as my thoughts tired I became tired and got off the bike to lie down under the leaves of a row of lombardy poplars. The traffic became a little fainter and Sudan less prominent. If I wasn't cycling I was eating and if I wasn't eating I was sleeping and if not sleeping was gently breaking wind. No more, no less, and no one seemed to care.

"Hey, wake up, wake up, come and have some lunch you must eat ......" I woke up drowsily as a teenage boy shook my shoulder to and fro, "Come and eat, come on, we've got something real nice," and he left me to follow, heavy with too much sun, I'd been asleep for two hours instead of five minutes and got up wearily to see what he wanted. At the end of the row of trees four lads were squatting around a stack of aluminium containers each holding a different dish. "Hi, I'm Hamed and I'm a tractor driver," he pointed to a brand new David Brown in the adjacent field. "Where you goin', where you go on yer cycle?" I sat for a moment waking up deliberating whether to tell him or not. He would almost certainly not understand why I'd committed myself to such a

journey, it would seem quite ridiculous to him, absurd. But then it **was** absurd and why **should** it be understood, though it's not more difficult than driving his tractor every day for the next fifty years. We ate a little meat and the three boys with him were younger, sweet-faced, obviously not understanding English. I told him. He thought for a moment, looked down at the ground and continued, "Why? Why you go, we have a little food and some work so life is good. It's not fair that you have to go there so far from your mother, I don't understand you." He carried on eating, from then on oblivious of me, disbelieving that I actually wanted to journey in such faraway places probably thinking me quite stupid. That divide had opened again and I was shouting across a canyon. My journey was integrated with a free way of life, of thinking, of doing; it was also immersed in bog standard glutinous phlegm where it was pointless saying 'No fair'. 'No fair' was no good. Why me? The saddest question in the world.

'Wadabrug' birds twittered above as I leaned back against the bark of a 'summut' tree. "Okay I'll stay here and stay in the shade, eat with you and live here," Hamed looked startled, "Sure, sure, but what will you do?" His question was answer enough and he offered me a mouthful of chewing tobacco. I said no, so he placed it between his lower lip and gums, easing it into position with forefinger and tongue. At that one of the boys threw a small black object at me and I caught it, holding in my palm a tiny black beastie, 'abu johran' they said, and it curled up in its hard outer cover. I thought it was dead but it moved and I jumped and the little boys laughed and I smiled. A stream trickled and gurgled nearby, its source being a square concrete tank with crystal clear water quite still. If only water could always be so clear, at home water retains fossilised clarity, here it dies within hours and at the bottom

stringly lengths of algae curled in a haven untouched, greenly soaking up the sun.

That afternoon I'd reached Wad Medani, a small bustling town well stocked with produce. I went into a grocers to buy more provisions and found a host of familiar items; Nescafé, Lyle's Golden Syrup, Heinz Baked Beans, and Vimto in its red and white striped cans. Small boutiques displayed a cluster of elegant goods, crammed to capacity as the dust rose in the road as I quickly passed by. A fruit juice and a sandwich and I was on my way, past the post office, the railway station and along a road that stretched as far as the horizon and further, to Senner.

At any given moment I expected Africa to show its fuzzy head, displacing Arabia and the Madhi for tall elephant grasses, tall elegant tribesmen and lions that softly pad-pad to roar loudly in the shimmering stillness of the African night.

Two days later I'd left tarmacadamed roads and I wouldn't see another until Uganda, once again sifting my way south through sand. Senner was a memory, Rabak a thought and the journey headed now towards Renk four days away and over 100 miles of atrocious dirt track.

The track was merely two deep ruts gorged by a lorry a day to keep the sand away. Riding was hard, the sand softer than the Nubian and occasionally hotter. All day my wheels scooped up the sand, whirled it around, sent it upside down to shower and drift back to the ground, only to be scooped up again. My tracks were slim, wavy and deep and I felt the fatigue wrinkle my face, moments of oldness mixing with the sweat and the sweltering Savanna. To my left a small herd of Thompson gazelle sprinted gracefully as one, running from sounds in the plains stalking their prey. A flock of coursers flew above, their long Dulux creamy white wings glistened cool with water, dipping and soaring, floating over dotted acacia, citrus blossoms and trunky baobab trees. And as I ploughed on relentlessly in a wilderness, I never felt alone although I was; it would seem too that the heat of the sun was melting the wax of my wings because I also was trying to fly.

After what felt like a four day penance I was tired, hungry and aching with the sun as I leaned my bike against the police station in Renk. A green-panelled facia covered with mosquito netting opened into a sturdy looking hardboard-topped counter. A policeman looked at my passport and papers — this is mandatory in Sudan — said they were in order and offered me overnight accommodation underneath the station verandah. I was directed to the river to wash, finding half the town's sailors shamelessly bathing between boat and quay. The heads of dead Nile perch floated in the flotsam, and spumey yeasty froth stuck to my ankles as a bucket of slops and sucked oranges were thrown out of a nearby port hole. They were surprised to see me, these strong men of Sudan. They probably wondered how such an emaciated-looking white man could travel so far, bathe in such a way and be seen in such a place.

Renk had little to offer. If the boats didn't arrive there was even less and as usual that night I ate beef, gravy soaked up with a little bread, and water from a tin can cup drawn directly from the Nile. Walking across the central market square towards a shop selling hot milk, a dirty dishevelled man came up to me and asked to shake my hand. "What's your impression of Sudan?" he said, looking over his shoulder as he spoke. I opened my mouth to answer when he grabbed my hand, shaking it firmly and conspicuously, and launched into a barrage of questions; "You like, you like people, friendly aren't they, you come again, you come here, you like me, what's your name?" His questions multiplied and quickened as if at any moment he would be stopped so there was no time for answers, just questions. What he was saying seemed to be based on a bizarre nonsense format superimposed over a conversation he was really having with himself. "You married, you have children, if not why not, what their names, oh how nice, are they black ......?" I laughed and invited him for a cup of tea, this funny little question man. I took him by the arm and his bloodshot eyes looked alarmed as he backed away like a beaten dog. "Tea, I'll buy you tea," I said but he told me he wasn't a beggar. I said I never thought he was and he became calmer, and as we walked towards the shop selling hot milk a rock hit him full on his leg and his face contorted with pain.

"Don't talk to anyone, we've told you before, you're mad." A voice came from one of three men sitting on a bench in front of a grocer's shop. "My dear friend he's mad and we'd simply prefer he didn't talk to you," and at that the largest, most obese, of the three came towards us and with a single calculated stroke struck the cringing man brutally with his foot sprawling him to the ground. "We would like you to think well of Sudan my friend, this is the reason we prefer you not to speak with mad people." He turned to the dishevelled man to laugh at his misfortune saying it was very funny and invited me to tea. I told him I didn't associate with mad men and said no. He walked away laughing and Mr Question Man ran away like the beaten dog he'd become and so I stood in the street in the dark, alone.

At that moment a group of street urchins surrounded me asking the usual questions and for the first time during this journey I felt terribly vulnerable. I thought they wanted to rob me, they probably did, and in the warm sticky darkness it wouldn't have been difficult. An overpowering feeling of claustrophobia blurred my thoughts and I starting sweating a viscous treacly clamminess; the air was stillborn and I was hardly able to breathe. Everything was dark and I saw no one in the street, tunnelled vision in a faraway land, but the boys touched me, my bike, trying to divert my attention to pick my pockets or slit open my panniers, goading me to anger and exploit violently the slightest careless action I felt inclined to make. I got on my bike and forced my way through this underworld circle, pedalling towards the police station and allowing myself no more time in Renk.

After five days cycling over 300 miles of rough Savana track the road suddenly turned to tarmac, broken and bitty, and there was an aeroplane landing strip on my right as I rode under a rusty metal banner inscribed with 'Malakal Welcome'. A long row of low brick wall buildings bore plaques and notices, 'Minister of this' and 'Department of that' and it was appropriate that all the vehicles used to repair the roads lay in a scrappy heap in the yard of the Ministry of roads and communications.

Cycling into town it dawned upon me I'd lost all idea of time and struggled even to remember what month it was. I had an address for a Mister Melvin, a United Nations delegate presently living here, he'd look after me. But on finding out it was Sunday and he wouldn't be at work I realised I'd never find him. Too tired to bother about anything now I rode on to the far side of town, away from people and dogs and questions and staring eyes and stopped where a burst standpipe trickled a little water under the shade of a eucalyptus. My legs were cramping with fatigue and my arms were blistering again; my head ached with the sun and as I got off the bike to lie down I was sick. My stomach filled with revulsion, dry heaving on nothing because it was empty, and kneeling down by the pipe I shook in the shade of the midday sun. Everything became blurred and white; the pipe, the road, the bike were all

TEN MAJOR DISEASES

Disease	Main Areas	Organism causing disease	Method of Spreading	Main Symptoms and Signs	Prevention or Treatment
Bilharzia	Egypt and North Africa, Sudan, North Ethiopia, Uganda, Congo, West Africa	Parasite	Life cycle in snails and water. Penetrates skin in water	Damage to involved tissue; bleeding from bladder and gut; in endemic areas much infection without signs	Kill snails; reduce contacts with infected water; chemotherapy
Cancer	All areas, especially 'ageing' population. Specific types found locally: i.e. jaw cancer in Ugandan children	Generally unknown: viruses sometimes responsible; radiation; chemicals	Non-communicable	Depends on part of body involved; cancer cells reproduce indiscriminately disorganizing tissues and spread to other parts of body, for example, lung to kidney or gut to liver	Surgery; cytoxic drugs; radiation
Dysentery (amoebic)	Tropics and Sub-tropics; North Africa	Parasitic amoeba	Contaminated food	Recurrent attacks; Mucus and blood-stained diarrhoea; usually painless	Improve sanitation; chemotherapy
Dysentery (bacillary)	Tropics and Sub-tropics; North Africa	Bacteria	Contaminated food and water; flies	Acute diarrhoea: colic and bloody mucus passed; dehydration; exhaustion. Mild cases are common	Improve hygiene; replace water loss; antibiotics
Filariasis	North Africa; West, Central and East Africa	Parasite worm	mosquito vector	Tissue inflammation and swelling generally involving legs	Elimination of vectors; chemotherapy
Leprosy	Nigeria, Congo, Central African Republic, Upper Volta, Benin (Dahomey)	Bacteria	Close contact for some time	Different types: 1) many bacteria; involving nasal mucosa, skin and nerves; lumps and areas of pigment loss or thickening in skin. 2) less bacteria; localized skin patches and nerves; loss of sensation, paralysis and gross deformities from damage to numbed areas	Immunization; chemotherapy
Malaria	Widely distributed; rare above 6,000 feet	Protozoan parasite (Several types: falciparum, vivax, malaria and ovale)	Mosquito vector; parasite migrates to salivary glands and infects at site of the bite	Symptoms depend on exposure of individual and community and type. Relapsing fevers; rigors; chronic or acute anaemia; enlargement of spleen with high mortality in non-immune infants; Blackwater fever	Eradication or control of the parasite by spraying breeding grounds or use of anti-malarial drugs
Trachoma	North Africa; Egypt; hot, dry areas with poor sanitation	Virus	Contact with infected cases and inadequate personal hygiene	Damage to the eye, initially the covering of the conjunctiva. Vessels spread over the cornea leading to loss of vision and eventually blindness, complicated by bacterial infection. In endemic areas mild or symptomless infections are common	Improve living conditions and water supply; reduce dust, dirt and flies; chemotherapy; surgical repair
Trypanosomiasis	A wide, patchy belt from Senegal and South Sudan to Okavango swamps in Botswana. Guinea, Ghana, Gambia, Nigeria, Sierra Leone, Congo and Cameroon	Protozoan parasite	Tsetse fly vector. Transmission depends on the number of man/fly contacts; animal reservoirs	Swelling at site of bite; Parasites in blood stream; later chronic, irregular fever, apathy, lethargy; involvement of central nervous system leading to confusion, falling asleep while eating and eventually coma. Time course varies	Clear areas of tsetse flies and reduce man/fly contacts; chemotherapy
Tuberculosis	Widespread	Bacteria	Direct infection; 'open' cases cough up bacteria in their sputum	Chronic disease; mild attacks protect in adult life; lungs affected, involvement leading to breathlessness, pneumonia, fluid in the chest and coughing up blood	BCG immunization treatment; Improved living conditions; Chemotherapy
Venereal Diseases Gonorrhoea	Worldwide	Bacteria	Sexual	*Male*—pain, discharge from urethra; swelling groin glands. *Female*—discharge from womb, infection of the tubes from the ovaries	Chemotherapy Treat carriers
Syphilis	Worldwide	Spirochaetes	Sexual	*Male*—sore at tip of penis. *Female*—sore at neck of womb. If untreated: rash; later involvement of brain and heart	High dose of penicillin; gonorrhoea and syphilis often treated at same time

Sleeping Sickness

Malaria

Bilharzia

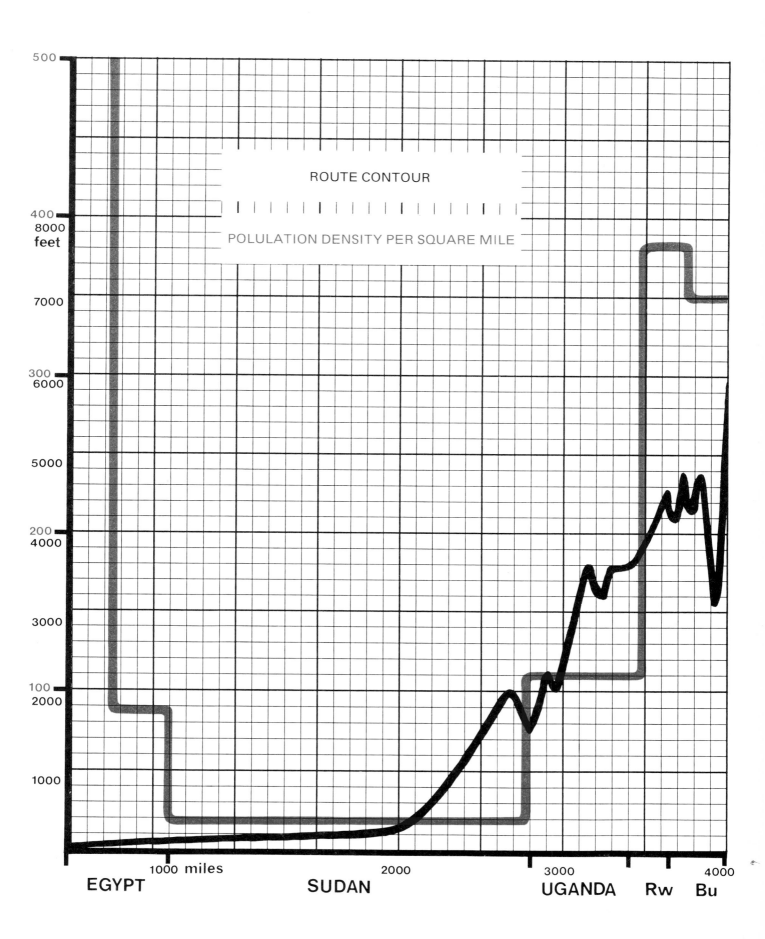

ROUTE CONTOUR

POLULATION DENSITY PER SQUARE MILE

500

400
8000
feet

300
6000

7000

5000

200
4000

3000

100
2000

1000

1000 miles   2000   3000   4000

EGYPT   SUDAN   UGANDA   Rw   Bu

devoid of colour, of smell, of life and I sat down languid and faint. Eucalyptus branches wavered in the breeze and I felt as though I was on a roundabout in a park back home. It would be Spring and grass would be lush, and in the distance I would hear children playing, clapping hands and laughing, little boys kicking footballs and little girls with pony tails playing house while the clouds twirled around above.

My dry tongue grated against the cracks in my lips which had started to bleed; even my eyes felt scorched, blinded by the sun, and I simply couldn't move. My mind wandered and it seemed ridiculous to think as I lay down by that fountain on parched grass that everything was so hard and that I myself and myself alone had made it so. That I'd tried to distance myself from all the things I knew and loved, to produce not only my own kind of human freedom but also the power of imagination. I imagined this journey possible and it became so. I also imagined it as it could never be because imagination essentially consists in representing things as they might be but are not. It would be human nature to abolish emptiness by filling in holes simply to possess the solidity of things, but here I was cycling into a hole and making it bigger.

The ground was hard, and like the princess and the pea I could feel every miniscular piece of grit underneath me. And as the clouds twirled to the vacant twittering of a warbler I realised I was looking for some kind of emotion to appease my apprehension. I wanted to stamp my foot to trample and destroy the unseen enemy; to run away from the 'face in the window' in the back of my mind; to look at my surroundings in such a way that casual laws would be replaced.

The experience of my emotions as I lay on the ground in a faraway fantasy on the other side of the world would be governed by a magic not applicable to ordinary ways of thinking, and for that I was still looking. It seemed to me that the borderline between madness and sanity is but a hairsbreadth, so too is the relationship fantasy has with reality and as I contemplated with nausea my own smattering of Africa, I closed my eyes trying to decipher my dream.

A Landrover pulled up allowing someone to lean out and speak, ''Are you all right, do you want a lift ...... take you to the canal if you like''. At that he got out and introduced himself to me as Mike and I couldn't believe my luck. I accepted and we put the bike on the roof. He switched on the engine, his girl friend, Jane, said ''Hi'' and we were away.

For most of the route between Renk and Malakal, 'corrugations' lined across the track. These raised bumps prevented my cycling more than ten miles per hour for fear of breaking a wheel. Everyone feared the corrugations; Lussinian was quite right when he told me in Khartoum how hard they were, and on a bike nearly impossible. It was fifteen miles to the Jonglie Canal, a French building project diverting the waters of the Nile away from the Sudd and they'd also built a smooth earth road all the way to Kongor, 113 miles North of Juba. ''Why don't you eat with us tonight and carry on alone tomorrow,'' suggested Mike, looking in his rearview mirror at me sitting in the back. I thanked him, it seemed a good idea to have a good night's rest with good food.

Within half an hour we'd reached the French camp site at the head of the canal, driven on to the road and accelerated to fifty miles per hour. ''The first time since Khartoum,'' said Mike and a moment later he pulled over as I dozed, to set up camp for the night.

Mike had long wavy hair, was a self-professed prodigy of the 'sixties, and when he wasn't humming 'It's a Beautiful Day' he was barnstorming around to heavy metal, boots fastened on tight. His favourite words were 'heavy duty' and described most things that happened to him. Beautiful sunsets 'he couldn't handle' and most occasions requiring 'heavy duty' exercises really 'did him in'. He had a passion for liquorice allsorts and had a friend called Herbert who was a vegan and furtively ate chocolate biscuits when no one was looking. ''We're going to Kenya,'' he said, as the fire he'd built burned brightly. ''Then Tanzania and across Zaire to the Cameroons, get a good price for the 'van' and fly home.'' We all looked into the fire. He'd still be fixing exhausts on to Cortinas if he wasn't here. Jane wouldn't even be doing that and as for me, it was one adventure at a time until one day they stopped and that would be the end of the road.

It was very dark now and Jane's chopped-up vegetable stew was bubbling nicely. Ants dropped from the trees onto my arms and I gently brushed them away on to the ground. I was never quick enough to see them fall, just land, as if they hadn't fallen at all but arrived at another point in space having taken no time to get there. A feeling of being there without having to get there, as if my expectation of the ant falling down to the ground facilitated that happening. It would certainly make a change if the ant fell upwards, just once. I tried to imagine tomorrow not existing, simply because I didn't want it to, or that England no longer existed because I wasn't there to witness it. Everyone there wouldn't see it that way, but would Africa exist for them? Here it was like outer space with a tinker's curse preventing anyone from imagining a former life, and as the smoke drifted up and up to the black cloud splattered sky I could have been on the dark side of the moon looking at the earth below.

''This is just too heavy to handle, it really does me in.'' And Mike looked out to the plains below as grasshoppers jumped and jigged around the curling flames of the

Nile Explorers II

In 1856, Burton had been given a grant of £1,000 from the Foreign Office and the patronage of the Royal Geographical Society. Speke was to be Burton's number two and the object of the expedition was to discover exactly the whereabouts of the Source of the Nile.

After five months of hard travel from Zanzibar off the East coast of Africa, Burton and his party reached an Arab trading settlement at Kazeh on 7th November, 1857. A month later they set off for Lake Tanganyika arriving at the slavery and ivory post of Ujiji on 13th February 1858 and both Burton and Speke were seriously ill. Burton had an ulcerated jaw and could take nothing but liquid food and Speke's childhood opthalmia had worsened considerably. On regaining his health, Speke set off leaving Burton behind, with a small group of porters and Baluchi Guards to investigate reports from the Arabs that an even larger lake than Tanganyika existed three weeks walk north of Kazeh.

Early in the morning on 3rd August, 1858 when he stood near Mwanza on the shore he saw an immense lake before him and wrote a strange thing in his diary, ''I no longer felt any doubt that the lake at my feet gave birth to that interesting river, the source of which has been the subject of so much speculation, and the object of so many explorers.''

Burton himself thought the source of the Nile lay further to the East in the vicinity of Mount Kenya and Mount Kilimanjaro, possibly even the Tanganyikan basin. Because of Burton's more reasoned approach to the journey and the intuitive, unscientific approach of Speke, a rift formed between the two. Burton wanted proof that the newly-named Lake Victoria was the source and Speke could offer flimsy geographical evidence together with strong conviction. In late September 1858 the expedition set off for the coast arriving in Zanzibar on 4th March, 1859; they had been away twenty-one months.

Both men were seriously fatigued, the younger man, Speke, recovered faster and whilst Burton continued his convalescence in Aden, it was agreed he return home on HMS Furious. It was also agreed that Speke would reveal nothing of the results of the expedition until Burton also returned home. They would thus part for ever.

Within a week of getting home it was known that a great discovery had possibly been made. Speke had gone directly to Sir Roderick Murchison, then President of the Royal Geographical Society, who was so intrigued

that he invited Speke to return to Lake Victoria and find its northern outlet to trace the river to Egypt. A sum of £2,500 was put at his disposal and a gaunt-looking Burton had been forgotten only to be replaced by another Indian Army Officer, Captain James Augustus Grant.

Grant was the perfect lieutenant, modest and self-effacing without a trace of jealousy, distrust or ill-temper, to such a degree that General Gordon thought him dull and a bore. Nonetheless he was a cool and steady man with great devotion to Speke. After journeying inland again as far as Uganda, they met Rumanika, King of Bunyoro, who was delighted to meet the two white men. Here Grant rested a bad leg whilst Speke set off to

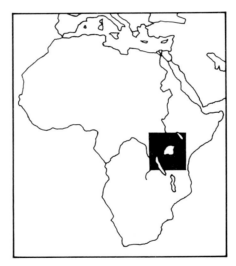

see Mutesa, King of Buganda. After gaining permission from the King to journey in his kingdom, Grant arrived and the two men set off for the Nile. On the way it was agreed that Speke temporarily proceed alone and not be delayed by Grant's bad leg. On 21st July, 1862 he arrived at Urondogoni, about forty miles downstream from the lake. After travelling upstream for one week Speke climbed a hill blocking their view to see a waterfall. The waterfall emitting from the lake was to be called the Ripon Falls.

All that remained now was to reach Gondokoro, on the opposite bank of the river from Juba, to collect £1,000 of Geographical supplies and meet Samuel Baker and his

wife who had come to look for them. Speke and Grant then sailed up to Khartoum and on arriving in Cairo cabled to London, 'Inform Sir Roderick Murchison that all is well, that we are on latitude 14°3' upon the Nile and that the Nile is settled.'

Samuel Baker was almost a caricature of the professional Victorian, the whiskered clubman figure, a practical down-to-earth-man who knew what he wanted and precisely how to get it. One, he wanted to have a little sport; two, he thought he might combine it with a little exploration, a journey up the Nile perhaps, maybe even to the source.

Baker had a lot of style taking delicacies from Fortnum and Masons, the best of equipment and a rack of guns made to his own specifications by the leading gunsmiths in London. Petherick, the British Consul in Khartoum, had been requested to search for Speke and Grant. Amidst reports, however, that Petherick was now dead, Baker had been asked to keep a look out instead.

After six months in Khartoum, Baker had acquired twenty-one donkeys, four camels, four horses, three sailing boats, ninety-six men and provisions for four months. Joined by a German explorer, Johann Schmidt, he set sail for Gondokoro. During this time he journeyed through the Sudd, a desolation of drifting reeds and ooze, a world of neither land nor water which covered in the wet season an area as large as England.

Schmidt died 'en route' and Baker and his wife were dreadfully ill and on hearing of Speke's reaching Gondokoro he decided to terminate his adventure. However, on hearing that Speke and Grant had not explored the Great Basin of the Nile, the Albert N'yanza, he set out immediately.

Baker's travels have great personal appeal; here is Allan Quartermain in his broad-rimmed hat with a young and lovely girl entering the jungles to face every conceivable hazard with marvellous determination. Their animals die and they are forced to ride oxen, their food supplies fail and they are reduced to eating grass. Having lain prostrate with fever for days, then weeks, they continue and hippopotamii overturn their boat; they're cheated and attacked by poisonous arrows and in the distance, in the faraway lands they hear a faint rumbling. Riding on the crest of the wind rolling down the hills to the banks of the river, they hear the beating of drums, war drums and the sounds of savage dancing. Baker and his wife reached Lake Albert and lived to tell the tale; isn't that the real spirit of adventure .....?

Explorers routes in East Africa

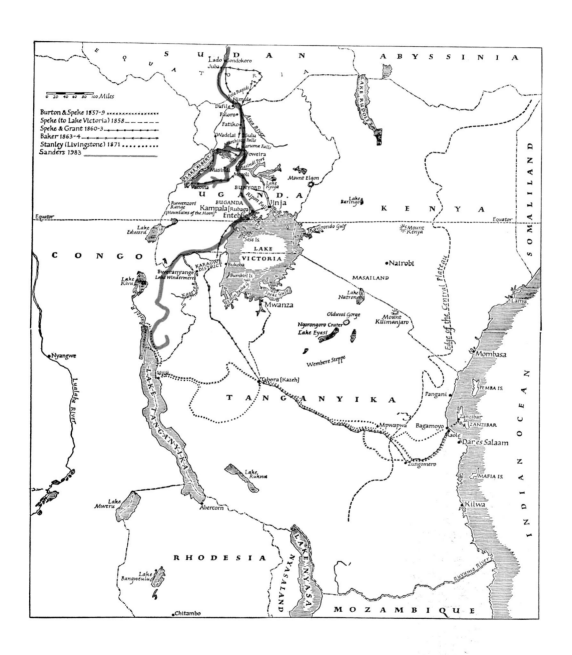

fire. I was dozing again, full-stomached and rested and a young stick-limbed hopper edged dangerously close to the burning embers lured by the warmth of the sticky yellow lights. Yellow fingers beckoned and called as he edged nearer and for the hopper these flickering embers were the bright lights of the world as he charged headfirst into the heat. No retracting now, he'd jumped, and the fire sizzled with glee and waited for another.

The following morning I said goodbye to Mike and his girlfriend and for two days pedalled South on smooth roads on the left bank of the canal to Kongor. I was well into Dinka territory and Kongor was a beautiful example of rural Africa. Bore holes had been sunk to supply sulphur clean water for drinking and also to irrigate the wheat to make the grain to feed the cattle to plough the fields to give the milk to feed the young. An elderly tribesman came up to me whilst I was drinking at a well, we didn't speak, he just watched. Tightly fitted brass bangles wrapped round his well-developed upper arms, around his wrists and ankles, while coloured pebbly beads hung around his neck. He didn't look in any way unkindly as he clasped a long slender brass pipe between strong white teeth. His eyes simply had no way of showing anything but genuine interest and concern and when a mouthful of water ran up my nose making me choke he smiled, I laughed and we shook hands as I said goodbye. A Dinka and a cyclist in Central Africa.

The road was now fair to good, a red clay-gravel sandtrack winding its way through masses of Acacia with their inch long thorns. Rocky boulder mountain outcrops started to mingle incongruously like my own blistered skin and as I descended towards the old pontoon bridge crossing the Nile into Juba a blue hand-painted piece of graffiti on a boulder caught my attention; 'Warrington R.C. Forever', ... haven't they done well?

Within hours I became nicely settled in Juba, a haven for mosquitoes and, so they say, a hell for men. I'd met a couple of overseas volunteers and they invited me to stay at their place, relax a few days, they said, away from the rest of the world, and I was the Sundance Kid holed up in Bolivia. But do I have to face the gunfire as well?

News drifted around and it augured badly for the journey; the Turkana in North West Kenya had robbed an aid organisation volunteer on his way to Nairobi and several of the river bridges had been washed away. The rains were beginning to fall and that would close North East Zaire to Kisangani. There was no alternative and my pathological fascination with a country at war would soon be examined.

Apprehensive of what was to come I drifted off to sleep restlessly tossing and turning. On the plains I slept deep and long cooled by a fresh blowing breeze, now sweat poured on to my pillow as I dreamed of a land of darkness and fire.

Diary

This is land where the earth had been scorched and buildings razed to the ground. Broken concrete foundations are scattered everywhere and rusty metal upright prongs stick out of the ground. There's a factory, or more a feeling of one, as blacksmiths pound on molten metal brickbats and a sinister-looking man wields more prongs to make them glow. His hairline is a widow's peak reaching down to his Roman nose and apart from the glowing metal, everything is in black except for a little blond curly-haired boy running after a puppy. Machinery pumps and clangs as the small boy tries to catch his pet but the dog is too excited and tears well in the youngster's bright blue eyes as they gambol in the midst of the misery of a nightmare.

UGANDA

The Lord is my shepherd; I shall not want.
He maketh me to lie down in green pastures: He leadeth
me beside the still waters.
Yea, though I walk through the valley of the shadow of death,
I will fear no evil: for thou art with me.

Psalm 23

Goodbyes verge on hellos. As soon as you say 'goodbye' to some- one there's always someone new to say 'hello'. It's always goodbye, hello, how-do-you-do, I'm fine, darling how are you?, it's so nice of you to come. Life is a party, Pimms and pink gins, apart from the gaps in between. Then I talk to myself knowing full well that some- one will listen. My own world in a goldfish bowl, alone with the wind. I'm a spaceman viewing a life that hasn't changed for centuries.

It took two days to reach Nimule, and I freewheeled to the border post feeling hot and bothered in the midst of a million acres of lion-stalked territory. Formalities were indeed informal; they were brisk without humour, some times unkind. Each time I approached border guards or soldiers on a deserted stretch of road I prepared myself for every possible reaction. Nothing ever hap- pened, but then once would be enough.

It was late afternoon by the time I passed guard houses blown up under the Amin regime — and that meant I was in Uganda. The sun was on the horizon and I knew I'd made a very serious error. To enter a new country without knowing the lie of the land is not easy, to enter a country like Uganda presents special problems. To enter at night was simply absurd.

The roads in Uganda are amongst the best in Africa, but this stretch to Atiak — only twenty miles away — ranked with the worst. Huge puddles stretched across the width of the track over twenty feet across and I had no choice but to wade through, knee deep in mud and fly-blown slime. Light was fading rapidly and the early evening smell of jungle was a rank fetid bouquet oozing from the tension between rot and genesis. I kept on walking, mile after mile, with each footfall sticking to the ground. A sweet afternoon turned into its smudgy burnt-out day and the obscenity of night. You could watch hot tropical sunsets that would change the way you thought about light forever. You could also step into places that are so grim that they turn to black and white in your head five minutes after you've gone.

I kept on walking, through the puddles, through the slime, caked in mud and from the trees a voice shouted out. ''Hey you, stand still and don't you move.'' I didn't even blink, ''What you do, you crazy? I just don't believe it'' and about fifteen soldiers sloped out of the jungle and out of the night. English is Uganda's official language and the moon reflected just a little on their black shiny faces. ''What you doin' here, this no place for you, man you crazy'' and a soldier of similar build to myself stepped forward. ''I'll have to have a look at your passport whilst my men search you ...... and you're on a cycle ...... where've you come from? I don't believe it.'' I told him and handed over what he wanted. Everything I had was examined. I expected delays and prying taunts, I expected a bloody nose, I expected what could feasibly happen yet it didn't, an unjust presumption.

''You're English, how nice. I spent several years studying at Eastbourne you know, lovely people.'' He was small, he was black and called Tom and he turned quickly to his men. ''Leave this man alone, he's a friend, he's English.'' then turned quickly to me. I released a deep pent-up breath and in a whisper to myself thanked him for his humanity. He was breathing in and breathing out, some kind of choice all by itself. As he looked at me nervously it was sad to see that he had one of those faces, I saw that face a thousand times ...... all the youth sucked out of his eyes, life had made him old and now he'd live it old. ''How I envy you your life. My English is good and I wanted so much to become a doctor. I'd like to do what you're doing but ......'' He paused and looked away meaning to finish but couldn't. ''You must go now, you will not be safe but if you are careful you will not be killed and that my friend is a good offer.'' I packed my bags and the soldiers, some were just boys, backed away and with gratitude and adrenalin I carried on without once looking behind.

Before I'd covered a mile I decided to get off the road and camp in the bush, alone in the darkness, and therefore safe. The area was a swamp and I hung up my mosquito net and laid my plastic ground sheet over moist earth, squelching in the drizzle that was now falling. My senses were working like strobes, free-falling all the way down to the essences and then flying out again in a rush to focus like colours secreted in a fog. I lay in the midst of an apocalypse with damp roots breathing; fruit sweated and in the swampy jungle stillness I could hear the heartbeat of tiny animals. I took in air that wasn't — more like 99% moisture — one clean breath was all I needed to dry sluice my anxiety and the backwater smell of my own body. I knew as soon as I closed my eyes I'd sleep and by morning I'd wake up tapped of all images, and to the sound of a macaw shrieking above. I closed my eyes and slept.

A mist covered the ground. It was cold and damp, it was very silent and it was morning. I got up, packed my sleeping bag and net and checked the bike to go. On my leg four leeches had fastened themselves securely, orange ones about three inches long and similar to those that had found me in Sumatra. Placing a little salt on each, their heads retracted from the bloodstream and curling up they fell off. Leeches inject an anti-coagulant into the wound they create and in a few moments my leg was covered in blood. Several plasters stemmed the flow a little and I carried on walking. By lunchtime I'd passed through eight road blocks and a convoy of Kenyan lorries bogged down in the swamp. I had my papers signed in a police station at Atiak and as everything was in order I could continue.

From Atiak to Gulu the road was unpaved but good and I made excellent progress for most of the day until I saw a sign saying Locar Seminary. Local people had told me that there were two American missionaries working there from the 'Sacred Heart of Jesus', so as it was getting dark I ventured inside the compound through a large green painted iron gate. With a squeak it opened and I pedalled slowly along a path with neatly trimmed edges lined with primrose, and lush bougainvillea mingled with the scent of chocolate orange from pea-pod sized cloves.

Walking towards me, a bespectacled man in a long white cassock introduced himself as Brother Elliot. I didn't have to explain I needed shelter for the night because he knew and led me to a small guest room with two single beds. There was a single chair by the wash basin which was next to a barred window covered with mosquito netting.

I changed into clean clothes and walked across the garden towards the dining room, passing the church where I heard the choir practising. Little boy sopranos trilled like nightingales in Berkeley Square and deeper tenor voices drifted with rain-laden wind. A pedal-operated organ resonated with a mellowness only found in churches and I remembered my own days in the choir. The 23rd Psalm, The Magnificat, and the day my dad told me at fourteen I was old enough to decide for myself whether to stay or not, so I left. These were the most beautiful sounds I'd heard for a long time and I turned to carry on, crunching feet on the gravel, to a rumble in the jungle and the smell of cooking fish.

''I'm Brother Joe and let me tell you my friend it's real good to see you fella.'' Brother Joe was Brother Elliot's associate, and the table was laid for dinner. ''Have a little mulberry wine, made it myself'' and Brother Joe poured me a glass as I tucked in to a huge

Tank on the Bombo Road. ''Can the world be read through the bloody thoughts of one man? A man whose despair is so great that anything at all which could alleviate sorrow would be used as a wedge to set against the bitterness''.

Near the bottom of the Murchison Falls in Uganda's Kabalaga National Park.

portion of Nile perch, courgettes and rice. Defrosted mango was dessert, piping hot milky sweet coffee to conclude and it all seemed so unreal as we retired to the living room to relax and digest the finest meal I'd eaten in two months.

In the corner of the room next to a carved ivory inlaid lamp standard, a 1950's Tone O Matic record player sat over a stack of albums. ''Oh we've got some good records'' said Brother Elliot, ''Reader's Digest Mail Order before the War; Mitch Miller and the Gang, Ray Conniff Singers and Rendezvous in Paris, I've even got a Bill Hayley one if I can find it.'' He couldn't so we settled for Sinatra. I made the mistake of saying to Brother Joe it was unbelievable because he always replies with, ''It's not unbelievable my friend, this is Uganda and in Uganda anything can happen''. How true that would prove to be. This was a real life hocus-pocus cigarette toking padre trucking forever on, right in the middle of nowhere. And that's cool.

For a few brief days when Brother Elliot wasn't introducing me to friends or showing me his geography classroom covered in magazine pictures, I would sit in his living room drinking sweet hot coffee, tune into the world service on the radio or flick through 'Time' magazine. Natassia Kinski was on the front cover, such a beautiful lady a million miles away, and I'd been on the road every day for thirteen months these last two years.

After Benedictine at 7.15 pm dinner would be served but a storm was brewing. I said goodnight and walked over to my room to pack my bags ready for another day on the bike and the first few drops of rain fell. Large bulbous splashes from dark billowing clouds and the wind rose and, as an ebb-tide, receded to blow stronger the next time. A flash of lightning appeared to detonate the crackle of thunder as a barrage of drum-fire grumbled in the air. I'd been asleep only to be awakened by the storm raging directly overhead, continuous sheet lightning turning night into day and the roar on the corrugated roof was deafening.

Diary 13th June 1983

Gulu — Stroboscope effect of flickering lights panning across the sky as if the intensity of the flash raised the tempo of the rain, the beat of the drum from the corrugated roof. The rain dribbled from the corrugations, motionless in the shivering light and a spider hangs grimly, swinging. It won't be long. This is a spider demolishing storm. The flashes made the mosquito netting look like the lines on TV screens. A cathode ray tube view of an electric storm and in the distance an empty field, the only empty space where direction is free from foliage. In the near distance with the emptiness behind, a tree raised her two arms and a woman is hanging. How I beckon her to come to me, how I beckon her to umbrella her way through the rain to tell me it's not her hanging in the tree, arms outstretched for all to see yet all will not see because it's her and me, the mosquito net the great divide, iron bars separate a lifetime. But there's a hole in the netting, maybe there's a hope, now all I have to do is gnaw at the iron bars with my teeth.

Alone in a storm in Uganda was the only occasion I could bring myself to write about my mother who was dying. A feeling of the extraordinary condensed on my sweaty arms, legs and sweaty face as I looked out of that window. When I eventually returned to Cairo in late July a letter awaited me telling of my mother's death. When I read the date she died, I knew I'd experienced something I couldn't explain — June 13th.

After a breakfast of three hardboiled eggs, Nile perch, home-made bread, jam and freshly roasted coffee, I said goodbye to people I may never see again and after six miles of red road reached the first stretch of tarmac since Rabak 867 miles ago. There would be tarmac roads all the way to the shores of Lake Tanganyika; 210 miles to Kampala, 354 miles further to Kigali and the final 300 mile sprint to the Source.

After changing £8 into Ugandan shillings at the Commercial Bank in Gulu I was pedalling with the wind on smooth black tarmac at over twenty five miles per hour. Brother Elliot had given me an address of a friend. Cross the river he said, twenty miles past the forest, past a church with no roof and turn left when you see a sign marked Kigumba Catholic Parish Church. Only a day's ride away.

The road had long uphill straights with slightly shorter downhill parts, I was climbing steadily to Lake Victoria, 3,500 feet on the Equator. School children of all ages greeted me with 'Good morning Sir'. They were beautifully dressed in white uniforms, with leather satchels slung over shoulders or perched delicately on heads. Ugandan children are amongst the most courteous, kind and intelligent people I have ever had the pleasure to meet. As the school bell rings, hundreds of children line the road walking as much as five miles to receive an education they feel privileged to be given.

Sitting by the side of the road eating a banana I contemplated Speke and Grant's epic adventures all those years ago. Likewise along with Baker I was actually riding on a similar one they used but I couldn't think for a moment that there was any real comparison between them and myself. I was quite alone apart from the odd army convoy rushing about wildly on detachment, quite alone thinking about Boy's Own Paper heroes when I noticed a chameleon. Mister Proteus, the chameleon, caught my eye as he walked towards me in a backward motion sort of way. Like a drunk with two left legs he seemed unsure of his gait, three steps back to hurl himself one step forward and the sun almost shone through his translucent green skin. Within minutes of walking on my hand his body turned mad red, a vermillion chameleon, and his long telescopic eyes darted out curses and thunder. I put him back on the ground by the side of the road and he slowly hurried away. Even chameleons get angry.

Lorries queue in the early morning mist on the Uganda/Rwanda border.

The sign of Kigumba Mission duly presented itself after an easy ninety miles and I knocked on the door of the Mission dispensary. "Ah, welcome. Yes, here you are, tea and biscuits. What about a shower? Oh, yes, bananas, we have lots of bananas. Sit down, I'm Father Giberelli and the house maids will assist you, must dash, got to dispense some medicine. Malaria, cholera ...... the usual." "But you don't know me" I said, but he was gone and he didn't care and the young serving girl asked me if I'd like a cup of tea. An hour later after I'd showered, Father Giberelli returned having given out his magic potions. "Ah yes, the fridge, it works better with the door open", and if he had a pipe he would have taken a small toke to contemplate awhile, but this little man had run out of spinach, and his bananas were bigger than his muscles.

"I went to Scotland once, spent three years there," and he pronounced Aberdeen 'Aberdeeno' with a full-blown Italian/Scottish accent. Like many missionaries, this Godly man from the Verona Fathers had little concept of time and even less need for it. He spoke of events fourteen years ago as if they were yesterday and he's been here ever since.

Father Giberelli lived and worked with Father Gino from Rome and at 8 pm we ate Nile perch, stuffed with tomatoes, macaroni soup, paw-paw and warm maize bread, all washed down with sweet hot tea.

After listening to the World Service at 9 pm the Brothers politely told me it was time for them to pray so I bade goodnight and stepped into the compound garden. Standing outside I could see a flickering lamp through a gap in the curtains, and I heard faint voices reciting. 'The Lord is my shepherd; I shall not want.' The channel to God was now open and they had fifteen minutes of scheduled prayer before it faded out or the lamp ran out of paraffin. The light wavered and they continued. 'He maketh me to lie down in green pastures: he leadeth me beside the still waters,' and I felt sad. Christians seem to do quite well in the face of adversity, in the face of a drunken soldier that could machine-gun them all over the dispensary wall. I couldn't help but wonder how many times one had to run in front of a machine gun before it became an act of cowardice. And as I lay on the verge of sleep I whispered to myself 'Yea, though I walk through the valley of the shadow of death, I will fear no evil: for thou art with me;' What I'd like to know is, who's thou?

The following day I stiffly rode on and within twenty miles had reached Lusaka, a pretty flower-lined village with purple and yellow pansies, peonies and sweet peas, orange and white geraniums crisply coloured in the sun. I rode through a road block manned by police, but though they allowed me through without any problem I was to be stopped in the centre of the village by a group of soldiers laughing and toting Uzi rapid fire sub-machine guns and waist-fuls of spare cartridges.

"Stop, I wanna ride your cycle," and a surly soldier roughly ordered me off the bike and tried to get on. He'd drunk an awful lot of millet home-brew, a grog-blossom of Africa which was strong enough to pickle the mightiest of men, and he fell off. Everyone laughed and his anger grew in proportion to his wounded pride as he tried again only to fall off hard on his shoulder, the bike clattered to the ground. His comrades were now hysterical with the fun and foolhardiness of such clowning and I held my sides the laughter hurt so much. Rearranging his machine gun on his shoulder he tried once more and hopelessly missed the pedals slipping on to his crutch and I winced. He tried again. The madder he became the more we all laughed and each time the bike clattered to the ground, each time he arranged his machine gun to try again. He was losing face and he knew it and that was dangerous fun as tears rolled down my cheeks. He got off the bike and threw it to the ground shouting with anger, hysterical anger and rage. Flaming passionate hatred of self abuse. He held his machine gun in position walking towards me, his face sickly contorted, and the laughing stopped by command. That's all I heard as my vision concentrated on straight-faced soldiers and I listened with dread to the sound of terminated laughter. My whole existence at that moment willed the situation back into farce with no effect and my panic seized the moment with a compromise. He walked in slow motion to give my mind time to discover an appeasement. I went to retrieve my bike and he pointed his gun at the bike next to me, finger on the trigger, and I looked over to the others. They were ordered not to move and they didn't. "Very funny. I press the trigger and your head comes off; very, very funny. We throw you in the bush and no one finds you, that very funny, yes. Mister. If you want to play laughing games I make you laugh real good, now go away before I get even madder." His eyes were bloodshot, unseeing, unthinking, unfeeling, uncaring, dead.

Ten miles further up the road I sat down in the shade of a huge strange bush, sitting knees up, resting my face on my arms. The gun had been eased away, an apology made. A glance of madness and I sat and sat and wanted to cry but couldn't as I felt so sick. Can the world be read through the bloody thoughts of one man? A man whose despair is so great that anything at all which could alleviate sorrow would be used as a wedge to set against the bitterness. To set against a war that eliminates the humble and nullifies the meek; that flogs the lowly and lets them soak up the pain, for one day they will inherit the earth. But there again maybe they won't.

That night I slept at Kassal, again with the Verona Fathers, and the next day I cycled along the Bombo Road, a ghostly strip of planet where people were too frightened to live. By lunchtime I'd arrived in Kampala and quickly found friends I'd met en route.

Thirty years ago Kampala was a beautiful city set in a hollow amongst valley hills. Kampala is still in the hollow of those hills and with a coat of paint would probably recapture its former beauty. Though now it decomposes and decays it still has a long way to go before all its charm is lost.

The tallest building in town is the twenty-two storey Ugandan Commercial Bank, opposite to which I breakfasted in a Kampala Coffee House. The western idea of furniture and fashion has translated here to mock pine wallpaper and ladies in dresses that occasionally fall above the knee.

There was also a religious fervour hanging in the air; on railings, stuck to car windows, pasted on boards sandwiched around little old men handing out leaflets and The Leadership Calendar with Christ on the Cross. Plaques had been sprayed with the consequences of sin and offered eternal redemption to those who surrendered to God. In the tea room over the Ugandan Bookshop, a yellowed edition of The Ugandan Times dated 27th September 1982 hung on the wall flapping under the strain of a whirling fan; 'Be faithful to God Muwanga ...... Uganda will not Collapse'. And that's official!

As I was looking around I noticed a composite Christ framed on the wall. I noticed too his negroid lips below a mongoloid nose and oriental eyes, all stuck on a Caucasian structured face. Wholesale Christ. Personally I wasn't too keen on the nose.

Diary

A conversation in Kampala.

Stucky hair way up there lacquered and embellished to the point where people remark on its thickness instead of its highlighting tones. Lonely sentiments so too are likewise noticed. "How strange of you to leave your homeland, what have we got to offer you that you yourself cannot get back home?" Nothing. "Do you enjoy leaving your family?" No. "Are you not married. Your job. Are you not here for a reason, why do you come here?" Not sure. I was trying to channel a trough of ideas away from the mainstream and enact them out in new territory, to wash my mind clean with abstract thoughts. It isn't a question of being happy, happiness simply doesn't enter into the scheme of things at all. Happiness is temporal at best and non-existent at worst. But then best and worst is as is dictated by the meaning of what is thought beneficial or not. I sit in a garden in Kampala, Lake Victoria to my right, a palm tree to my left and drizzle scrapes away at humid air. The rain keeps falling, the journey will continue. A journey that is an enactment of will and desire which transcends itself to the point of uncertainty, and I thought it would be the other way round. I thought that the deeper into the heart of darkness one trespasses, the more likely answers to questions would unfold. Now the answers demand to know the questions and I can't think of a question that doesn't necessitate an answer.

Drinking in the coffee house I'd been told that the Bombo Road was one of the most dangerous in Africa, huge massacres were common, villages violated, raped and pillaged. And as I looked around, the western influence was still here as a residue of a former colonial upbringing. Men wear white shirts and grey suits whilst the ladies harbour blouses and skirts and first class leather shoes. I sat next to a beautiful girl, also drinking coffee. She hadn't any wrinkles, her skin was pulled tight over her forehead and high cheekbones gave her acute features. The lack of character lines

coincided with her blackness which seemed to absorb features as white skin reflects them. But foreheads are strong, prominent even, and her hair was braided into contortions to form a hydra bun on her head and she was absolutely beautiful. We spoke a few words as a biscuit crumbled on to her harebell blue dress — then she left and I knew it was time also to set off on the last stage. I was destined to enter a strange land of Tangerine trees and Marzipan bees, two-headed monsters and savages that eat white men alive.

It would be wrong to say that Livingstone and Stanley were my boyhood heroes. I hadn't had an explorer's upbringing and I was never quite sure how much significance these two great men had in opening the eyes of the world to Africa. I certainly never thought that I'd be visiting the very places that mean so much in the historical sense.

David Livingstone was born on 19th March 1813 at Blantyre in Scotland. Livingstone did not have a privileged upbringing as did Burton or Speke, Grant or Baker, his was distinctly pious, poor and hardworking with a great zeal for education and a sense of mission. Livingstone was reared as one of seven children in a single room at the top of a tenement building for the workers of a cotton factory on the banks of the Clyde. His parents had a background of militant Presbyterianism and it goes without saying that both were poor. Brought up in the Calvanist faith he automatically had great discipline of mind and body which would fit him for his African career.

Because of the opium war [1839-42] his initial plans to go to China were dashed so with the advice of Robert Moffat, a Scottish missionary in South Africa, Livingstone set sail for South Africa at the end of the year and arrived in Cape Town on 14th March 1841. For the next fifteen years he travelled incessantly, gaining converts in the difficult Kalahari country and in 1844 was badly mauled by a lion. This injury to his left arm would affect him for the rest of his life, never able to support the barrel of a gun.

A year later Livingstone married Moffat's daughter, Mary, who accompanied him on many of his journeys until she was forced back to Scotland to support their family.

After making his famous statement in 1853 ''I shall open the path into the interior, or perish'', he journeyed without rest in Zambesi; the Boer territory; Mozambique, leading expeditions, lecturing in Britain and generally spreading the word.

Whilst there was no doubt as to the integrity and determination of Livingstone as a solitary explorer, his ability to lead occasionally came into doubt. His Zambesi expedition was recalled by the British Government in 1863 when it was clear Livingstone's optimism for the development of the area was premature. So too his very greatest wish to find the source of the Nile was never really feasible as he grossly miscalculated Speke's findings to his own detriment.

Livingstone believed the Luabela leading into the River Congo would provide all the answers and after an arduous crossing from Mikindani on the East coast of Africa, some of his followers deserted him spreading rumours that he was dead in order not to be punished.

The nearest he got to the source was the northern shores of Lake Tanganyika in February 1869 and then, as a failing and sick man he returned to Ujiji on 23rd October 1871. The arrival of Stanley and fresh supplies of food and medicine decided him not to return to England as Stanley wanted, and obsessed with his quest to find the Nile's source, his illness overcame him.

On 1st May 1873 at Chitambo's village [one of his most faithful servants] he was found dead, kneeling at his bed as if in prayer. His heart and viscera were removed and buried in Africa and his embalmed body was carried for nine months to Zanzibar. It was taken to England and in a great Victorian funeral, buried in Westminster Abbey on 18th April 1874.

Livingstone

Henry Morton Stanley was born on 28th January 1841 at Denbigh, North Wales, the illegitimate son of John Rowlands and Elizabeth Parry. His mother then left him to the care of her father, Moses Parry, and he grew up in the charge of unwilling relatives and the St. Asaph workhouse.

Stanley was one of very few explorers who didn't have an aristocratic upbringing and the humiliations of institutional life along with his mother's continued neglect, left deep marks. Consequently at fifteen he ran away to sea, sailing as a cabin boy from Liverpool to New Orleans, Louisiana, where he landed in 1859. His father, now living in America, cared for him briefly before dying abroad on business, but at least young Stanley recognised one person loved and believed in him. In his own prosperous middle age he too adopted a son.

For some years Stanley led a roving life; seaman on merchant ships, a journalist in the early days of frontier expansion and a soldier in the American Civil War. Twice he visited his mother in Wales only to encounter the same indifference she had shown him since birth.

Stanley was in Madrid covering the Spanish Civil War for the New York Herald in 1869 when James Gordon Bennet jnr, his editor, summoned him to Paris and commissioned him to ''find Livingstone''.

Little had been heard of Livingstone after he left for the interior of Africa in 1866 to explore the central African lakes and ascertain the source of the Nile, he was thought to be near Ujiji on Lake Tanganyika. On 21st March 1871 Stanley set sail from Zanzibar for the interior, reaching Ujiji in November, where he found Livingstone ailing, short of food and medicine and a famous greeting was endorsed, ''Dr. Livingstone I presume?'' Stanley referred to missionaries contemptuously as 'mish's' but his respect for Livingstone was great and his desire to gain a newspaper scoop was equalled only by his love of the man himself. Stanley arrived back in Zanzibar in May 1872 leaving Livingstone to search for the source of the Nile further west, a region it was proved later to be watered by the Congo.

When Livingstone died in 1873, Stanley returned to Africa adorned with society awards, and it would be he who would vindicate Speke's intuitive recognition of Lake Victoria as the major source of the Nile at the same time repudiating Burton's criticisms. In 1876 he circumnavigated Lake Victoria in his boat 'Lady Alice' during which time several violent skirmishes with natives raised eyebrows back home. Stanley's brash, forceful adventurism was a bridge between the old school and the new, the seeds of unpopularity were to be sown. Stanley also circumnavigated Lake Tanganyika and found no connection there with the Nile. He likewise made positive association with the mist-covered Ruwenzori range and Ptolemy's mountains of the moon.

Stanley was instrumental in opening up the Congo for trade, for King Leopold II of Belgium, his sponsor. He launched steamers in the Congo, built roads, cleared jungle and his perseverance in the face of difficulties earned him the title from the men who worked with him of Bula Matari — 'the rock breaker'.

In later life he married Dorothy Tennant on 12th July 1890 and they adopted a son, Denzil. Having been naturalised an American in earlier years he once again reverted to British citizenship in 1892 and sat in Parliament as Liberal Unionist member for North Lambeth from 1895 to 1900. In 1899 he was awarded the Grand Cross of the Bath and humble illegitimate John Rowlands junior became Sir Henry Morton Stanley. Stanley died in London on 10th May 1904 and was buried at Pirbright after a service in Westminster Abbey.

and Stanley

THE SOURCE

Tangerine trees and marzipan bees and sweet smelling waters
of white curds and whey.
Mountains of honey and fish that look funny, flying by night
and disappearing by day.
And isn't it strange in the distance I see ......

Everything was shrouded in mist. Heavy air ladled down the steep mountain slopes, and droplets of dew glistened in the early morning dawn shivering with the gentle breeze. I woke up soaked to the skin having spent another night in the hills.

There would be no more mosquitoes now, it was too cold, and as the mist dropped off my knees I packed the few possessions I still had and pedalled away from the outskirts of Kabale.

Visibility was down to ten metres as more cloud was shovelled over the edge. The road hung on the side of a mountain, a wall of foliage ruffled windily on my right with a near vertical ravine on my left. On both sides of the spooky cobbled road walked hundreds of children on their way to school, even in the hills the politeness and courtesy was there and as another drop of wet air condensed on my face to percolate off my nose, down my cheeks, I remembered that I was still in Uganda.

I was cycling uphill to the Rwandaise border, fifteen miles of moderate climb to Gatuna, and when I arrived I found somewhere to eat straight away.

Breakfast was in a shack called the Godown Hotel, coffee and tough leather-boot textured doughnuts to pad out the belly. Most of the diners were big Kenyan lorry drivers on their way to Sudan, or Burundi via Kigali, and what they hadn't done in life didn't seem worth doing. ''I know that road you bin on, man it sure is a bad one.'' He was referring to the stretch between Nimule and Atiak. ''Lived in that swamp three weeks before I could dig out the lorry, you know what I mean?'' I did.

The mist was lifting gently and I could see Kenyan trucks strung out half way across Rwanda. Rwanda is not very big. The customs official was two hours late so this pocket of Africa would be closed until he'd finished his breakfast. He also had to take his daughter to school which naturally took precedence over affairs of state — even if it was just simply to open up the country! When he did arrive, formalities were laid back and friendly. I told him he should get up earlier, he said I should stay in bed longer. Such is Africa.

I crossed the border post in Rwanda, passed trucks ticking over eager to go, and the mist had dissipated showing deep valleys dissected by streams cutting sharp ravines hundreds of feet to the valley floor. Cash crops of tea and coffee formed plantations on flat ground, grassland euphorbias stuck grimly to the steep-sided slopes but the road was excellent and it was only sixty-two miles to Kigali. The sun started to shine and I didn't feel quite so damp.

The plantation pickers waved as I passed by, old men stood and stared and children chased me until breathless. The route undulated and wound round a hill-side, puffy clouds flopped about in blue sky as swallows glided and paused and turned and dived. And as I lunched on boiled banana mash and gravy, Ugandan

Matoke, little girls would sit next to me in my wooden shack restaurant, swinging their legs coyly, wanting to hold the hand of the first white man they'd seen.

Kigali is built on the top of a hill, all roads go up or down steeply. After sending a message to London from the Air France office, I freewheeled around to look for somewhere to stay. When I'm in the vicinity of people someone invariably invites me to stay at their home, be it hut, house or mansion, and I live for one night as part of the family. In return they want nothing but an exchange of ideas and a change of view, someone new with whom to talk and to alleviate their particular boredom of the moment. I'd heard that the Catholic Mission gave bed and breakfast for a nominal fee and was just about to set off when two lads trundled past in a Landrover with a GB sticker on the back. They stopped outside the Rwanda Commercial Bank and I caught up with them to say hello and we agreed to set up camp together in the grounds of the French cultural centre.

By nightfall a small fire was burning and Julian was cooking potato stew as Len looked after the tea. Both lads had built up their van to try and make it to South Africa, work awhile and then come back. Compared to me they were really travelling in style. Avocado pear sandwiches for starters, followed by well-boiled potato-bean stew. Dessert was a whole banana each followed by jam and bread with lemon tea to finish.

Sometimes between villages I wouldn't eat anything more than bread for two or three days. Did they really eat like this often? ''Oh no, not all the time,'' said Julian, ''Normally we have mangoes for dessert but we've got to put up with bananas for the present.'' As the fire started to burn out, its embers reminded me of that kamikaze grasshopper all those miles ago, edging into the flames to begin a brand new life, reincarnated as a dead grasshopper. Len made me a last cup of tea and I slept early so as to be ready for tomorrow with a hope of reaching the Burundi border.

Kigali was too modern to explore. Whatever the reasons for such relative opulence it appeared as a clean, bustling town-size city. In my mind it was abstraction itself to have street lights in the heart of Africa, the equivalent of straw huts being erected on Blackpool beach. By 9 am I had breakfast with the lads and as they had to wait for some money to be telexed from home I promised to see them in Bujumbura.

All morning I climbed, up and up and I felt so good, almost inspired as I weaved between scattered copses of larch and evergreen bands of white birch. Loose leaves from the plantations blew across the road as if by an Autumn breeze and this I convinced myself was contentment. For the first time on the journey all my anxiety had been blown away, all my fears of failure grounded. I was but three cycling days away from a dream that had for so long become a prodigious obsession. The journey had become everything I'd ever wanted.

Stopping at a little cafe at the top of the plateau at Giterama I asked for some meat and a cup of tea. The official language is French with very little English spoken. Immediately I sat down, twenty village elders sat down next to me, leaning forward as if to smell me. Perhaps here they can smell the attitude of a man relying less on the white man's smile. The sweet refrain from a monastery garden eased out of a radio fastened to the wall. I wanted to sleep but each time I tried one of the men prodded me with a question, "Va tu et," I would hear in pigeonised English and the scent of a banana distillery tweaked the air. I told them Butare and after my meal got up, left, and hoped at least to reach the border if not today perhaps the next.

Fourteen miles later I reached the outskirts of Butare. Very little of Rwanda was to compare with capricious Cairo. Never was I to be haunted by my ghosts in Sudan or so nauseated as in Uganda. Life for me here was not one of extremes but of consistent mediocrity, and, so far from home in the heart of darkness, that seemed on reflection an absurd thing to think.

I stayed that night with a group of Belgian ex-patriots I'd met by chance. Claude's home was a culture-pot of stray art which he'd picked up on his travels. Curtains fashioned in Israel, ebony statuettes from the Ivory Coast and posters depicting the Festival de l'Erotisme at the Bastille. He loved English landscapes and had a series of Bill Brandt photographs on his living room wall; Stonehenge Under Snow and Gulls Nests on the Isle of Skye. What struck me most as I chatted in the midst of a party was partly the poster of Charlie Chaplin sitting grainily on a doorstep next to a little lost boy, but moreso the fact that Claude had chosen to position a young, demure Greta Garbo alongside; isolated, aloof, unique.

Next morning after a bread roll and coffee I cycled out of town. There was a seventeen mile mountain slope to climb, a seven mile descent and then the Burundi border. All the way up the vegetation became increasingly more sparse as wet wooded savanna stretched high towards misty blue and the sky, littered with bilious clouds, drizzled.

[Opposite page]
Bush children on the slopes of Rwandaise hills.

Typical pastoral scene in Rwanda, tea plantations as far as the eye can see.

"Well hello there man, don't tell me you bicycled from Europe 'cos I won't believe you." The border guard had an amazing sense of humour and I told him I'd biked from Manchester. "I don't believe you because that sure is a long long way .... anyhow where's Manchester?" He stamped my passport and I asked him how far it was to Bujumbura. He looked up at me, handed me back my passport, paused and smiled, "Seventy miles and 402 yards".

I pedalled the whole day almost without eating, excited and anxious to catch my first glimpse of Lake Tanganyika. Long deep descents plummetted out of the clouds and soaring climbs wound high into blue sky with groups of children dropping branches of bananas or bags of tea to race after me. I only had to slow down a little, turn around and scowl, and a screaming, howling animal cry would tumble out of a little black face to turn away in abject horror!

Burundi is a mountainous country lying across the dividing crest of the Nile and Congo watersheds over 6,000 feet high. Here amidst the tropical forestry, the drizzle and the altitude, the air was cool and I put on a jumper ready for the long fifteen mile descent to Bujumbura.

Round the corner and nearly close enough to touch, a mysterious expanse of water stretched and shimmered to the opposite shore and the far distant mountains of Zaire. Lake Tanganyika.

A couple of local lads freewheeled with me, braking into corners accelerating out of them, a deep breath at every bend, while the lake lapped and slopped as the sun began to set.

Claude had given me an address of an English teacher, Roger, who had family in Bruges. When I eventually found him, he and his girl friend, Francoise, made me very welcome. They had a spare house and said I could stay as long as I wished; as I badly needed the rest I decided to stay a few days.

I was one day away from the source of the Nile but in a strange way I was no longer anxious to get there. The journey in the metaphysical sense would then be over and returning home would be as a matter of course. I wanted also to savour the feeling of achievement that had become important to me; an achievement as great as rowing the Atlantic, no greater than making someone feel special on a grey, rainy day. Achievement is the Pyramids or the beauty of Cleopatra; it's the grace of the Peregrine Falcon and a hopper that can never say no. It's Ugandan children, uniforms beautifully crisp and white; it's a greengage chameleon trying to cross the road.

The waves broke on the beach at Tanganyika sifting through the sand. Picnic-time at Tanganyika; sun-shades, sail-board and my second day of rest. The expatriot community were mainly Europeans on Government projects and they licked ice creams en masse. How often I'd thought of this day, relished it getting closer, until the scent of cold drinks and chocolate started to melt and dribble before me. The horror of realising that I could no longer be placed into a slot to be jig-sawed into other peoples lives appalled and yet pleased me as much as would a fool on the hill.

I couldn't stay long. After a few days mooching around a town I didn't know, sailing on the lake and eating 'bread and honey' I packed my bags with imagination and flair (bananas, dates and boiled eggs) in preparation for the following day's ride. That night I sat on the beach looking out to tiny fires blazing and twinkling on the distant Zarois shore. As the lake lay sober and solemn, serene and still, the world that I had come to know had now become a world of make-believe and fantasy. Tangerine Trees and Marzipan Bees; sweet smelling waters of white curds and whey; of Mountains of Honey and fish that looked funny, flying by night and disappearing by day. And isn't it strange in the distance I see ......

I left Roger after breakfast. The road was good, the sun was warm and the wind right behind me. Conditions were to be perfect all morning as the dappled sea to my right reflected stippled light sprinkled to tint a deep burial blue.

Frangipani and Fuschia spotted the side of the road and clumps of citrine-coloured vetch scattered a jasmine hue down to the water's edge. Fishermen snoozed in the shade as their boats tilted on one side, drying on sunny warm sand. Women repaired nets as young boys loaded the bait for the evening sail. A heron drifted just above me and if birds could talk he would have remained quiet. Quiet so as to frame slow suspense. And as dry wisps of cinquefoil blew in the wind, I left the main road at Rumonge to head inland towards Bururi.

The smooth road turned to a cobbled track with such a steep gradient I had to change into my lowest gear — climbing over rounded stones and gravel, jammed with Burundi clay. The mountains sticking out of the deep valley below were like the colossal humps of coloured dinosaurs, covered in green burial gowns laid out to graze. Fields hung on the sides like strips of 'elastoplast' and the fragile remnants of a tree lay stark naked, denuded by the wind. As the road went higher and steeper, the odd mountain stream rushed across the road en route to the mountain bottom. A little boy sat on the crumbling remains of a wall. Whilst I stopped for a drink and a handful of dates I stood watching the little tattered fellow with his sniffly nose and liquid running eyes. Behind me the valley stretched 6,000 feet to Tanganyika and the wind whined through rustling grasses while a bullfrog took a deep breath and croaked.

Diary

A pluralistic universe with African acoustics. Here I am high upon high on the fringe of hair trigger eternity. The heart of Africa in a cataleptic state. Beneath the surface an explosion is pending, requiring only the advent of some utterly minute detail, something microscopic but thoroughly unpremeditated ...... then the detail coagulates, crystallizes like frost on a window pane free and fantastic in design but determined by the most rigid laws.

After a short rest I left the little boy and he watched me wind my way on to the plateau; the road was better now and thirty minutes later I reached the Chinese road. The Chinese were building a road along the length of Burundi, from Bujumbura to the Tanzanian border — this particular twenty mile stretch went straight to the pyramid next to the source. A German explorer, Dr. Baedaeker, built his pyramid to commemmorate Nile explorers and it wasn't far away.

All the time I wound higher and the air became cool, crisp even, and the unpaved red shale surface flicked and clinked against my bike. The landscape had become English; lush green pastures with imported Friesian cattle. I wanted to go up to one and pat her on the head as if to say, it's nice to be back, it's nice to be home, but I didn't.

Streams trickled and gurgled and clumps of silver birch glistened in the wake of a watery sun which shone just enough to give patches of purple heather highlighting tints. Peat bogs were, as ever, black and stodgy but on the fringe of good fashion. Peat and heather are classic components of country life; deerstalkers and Burberry; Aquascutum and plus fours.

I was restless and carefree, anxious and expectant, apprehensive nervous. In the distance I could make out a glistening speck

on a hillock and as I got closer it turned into the pyramid. Local boys ran with me as I rode, all the way to the base of the hillock itself. A moment later and I was standing next to a grey pieced-together cairn, cemented into perpetuity. The hills of Tanzania were in the near distance to the South and East; Zaire to my West; 4,165 miles of hardworn route to my North. I was on top of the world looking down on the plains below, the chatter of children mixing with the wind.

Diary

> *Being up there with the wind, there was a sense of being calm, tranquil; a journey completed, and whatever should happen or should have happened bears no relation to the present. The present is the pyramid. It's the wind I think, that creates a few moments of timelessness, an about-turn, a point where one just about begins to return without having yet stopped moving forward and the hustle and bustle of the getting here is forgotten.*

I climbed off the hillock and pushed my bike over to a clump of trees two hundred metres away on the other side of the road to sift my way down on a track worn bare by villagers treading their way to collect water for the day. A concrete bay clasped a metal pipe which trickled water into a stone basin. A concrete bay and a metal pipe is the source of the world's longest river, the source of the Nile.

I sat down on a stone to finish off my food, drink the purest water I'd seen for months and go over the journey, week by week, adventure by adventure, country by country, thought by thought. I knew the whole project was absurd, a romantic notion that had no relevance to ordinary life other than on the fringe of imagination, on the fringe of everyone's particular madness in the hidden back-water abyss of redundant freethinking minds.

"All morning I climbed, up and up and I felt so good, almost inspired as I weaved between scattered copses of larch and evergreen bands of white birch. Loose leaves from the plantations blew across the road as if by an Autumn breeze and this I convinced myself, was contentment. For the first time on the journey all my anxiety had been blown away, all my fears of failure grounded. I was but three cycling days away from a dream that had for so long become a prodigious obsession. The journey had become everything I'd ever wanted."

A butterfly flew around me and settled on the ground, sunning its black wings, enjoying its day of life. Within an instant she had closed her wings and become a sliver of the thinnest of lines, to form the shadow of a line on the sandy earth. I was sorry because with the help of the angle of the sun she had disappeared; there again maybe she really had disappeared. So too her one day of life could be thought absurd and yet it wasn't, because for one day her beauty would be seen and understood. And through all the slime and debris and the uliginous sloblands of the world I'd rather see one day in the life of a butterfly than not see it at all. Maybe that's the purpose of the journey. Out of days, weeks, months of asinine clowning adventurism there is one day that makes it worthwhile. One day of inspiration that doesn't provide answers but the realisation that the questions were wrong in the first place. That within the creeping insufferable tears which are shed in the midst of adventure, there will at least be brief moments of wonder onto which one can cling. That butterflies remain so beautiful and the sound of trickling water never stops; that on the crest of the breath of a wind the ingredients of dreams will always be carried and that peat bogs and heather and saffron-misted moons will always last forever.

"People I'd meet would take it for granted that I was articulate, ask me if I minded, but usually the questions were political, square, innocent, they already knew what they wanted to hear, I'd practically forgotten the language. Some people found it distasteful or confusing if I told them that, whatever else, I'd loved it there too. And if they just asked, 'What was your scene there?' I wouldn't know what to say either, so I'd say I was trying to write about it and didn't want to dissipate it. But before you could dissipate it you had to locate it, Plant you now, dig you later: information printed on the eye, stored in the brain, coded over skin and transmitted by blood, maybe what they meant by 'blood consciousness'. And transmitted over and over without let-up on increasingly powerful frequencies until you either received it or blocked it out one last time, informational Death of a Thousand Cuts, each cut so precise and subtle you don't even feel them accumulating, you just get up one morning and your ass falls off."

Quote: 'Dispatches' by Michael Herr

The Source

of the Nile

© Nick Sanders, November 1983
ISBN 0 946940 00 2 (card covers)
ISBN 0 946940 04 5 (case bound)

Production by Mopok Graphics, Glossop, Derbyshire
Photography by Ian Woollams, Studio 2, George Leigh Street School, Manchester
Design by Ray Eatock, 'A' Design, Manchester
Printing and Binding by Heanor Gate Printing Ltd, Heanor, Derbyshire
Distribution by Transport Publishing Company, Pikes Lane, Glossop, Derbyshire
Published by Nicholas Sanders Publishing, PO Box 17, Glossop, Derbyshire, SK13 8AX